£4.95

POCKET GUIDE

to

The G.I. Factor

and

SPORTS NUTRITION

Helen O'Connor

Associate Professor Jennie Brand Miller

Dr Stephen Colagiuri & Kaye Foster-Powell

GW00729209

Hodder & Stoughton

A Hodder & Stoughton Book

Published in Australia and New Zealand in 1997
by Hodder Headline Australia Pty Limited,
(A member of the Hodder Headline Group)
10-16 South Street, Rydalmere NSW 2116

National Library of Australia Cataloguing-in-Publication data

Pocket guide to the G.I. factor and sports nutrition.

ISBN 0 7336 0500 1.

1. Diet therapy. 2. Diabetes – Diet therapy. 3. Dietetics.
4. Food – Carbohydrate content. 5. Athletes – Nutrition
I. O'Connor, Helen.

613.2

Printed in Australia by Griffin Press

CONTENTS

INTRODUCTION

Sports nutrition is a new and dynamic science dedicated to unravelling the key nutrition factors that boost sports performance. What you eat does make a difference to your performance. The trick is getting into the right eating routine, keeping up to date and ignoring the confusing nutrition myths that abound.

This book looks at a new key factor: the G.I. factor. Australian researchers were the first to see the potential in applying the G.I. factor to athlete's diets to enhance sports performance. This guide shows you how to use the G.I. factor in your own diet to boost your sports performance. When you pop this pocket book into your training bag, you'll have

- a quick quiz to help you assess your current eating habits
- refuelling hints at your fingertips
- case studies that provide you with fun, easy and practical ways to eat your way to better performance
- G.I. tables of foods including sports drinks plus their fat and carbohydrate count

What you eat does make a difference to your sports performance.

IS YOUR DIET FIT FOR PEAK PERFORMANCE?

Take the diet fitness quiz and see how well you score. It's a good idea to use this quiz regularly to pick up on areas where you may need to improve your diet.

1. Circle your answer.

Eating patterns

- I eat at least 3 meals a day with no longer than 5 hours in between — Yes/No

Carbohydrate checker

- I eat at least 4 slices of bread each day (1 roll = 2 slices of bread) — Yes/No
- I eat at least 1 cup of breakfast cereal each day or an extra slice of bread — Yes/No
- I usually eat 2 or more pieces of fruit each day — Yes/No
- I eat at least 3 different vegetables or have a salad most days — Yes/No
- I include carbohydrates like pasta, rice and potato in my diet each day — Yes/No

Protein checker

- I eat at least 1 and usually 2 serves of meat or meat alternatives (poultry, seafood, eggs, dried peas/beans or nuts) each day — Yes/No

Fat checker

- I spread butter or margarine thinly on
  bread or use none at all   Yes/No
- I eat fried food no more than once per week Yes/No
- I use polyunsaturated or mono-unsaturated
  oil (Canola or olive) for cooking.
  (Circle yes if you never fry in oil or fat)   Yes/No
- I avoid oil-based dressings on salads   Yes/No
- I use reduced fat or low fat dairy products   Yes/No
- I cut the fat off meat and take the skin
  off chicken   Yes/No
- I eat fatty snacks such as chocolate,
  chips, biscuits or rich desserts/cakes etc.
  no more than twice a week   Yes/No
- I eat fast or take-away food no more
  than once per week   Yes/No

Iron checker

- I eat lean red meat at least 3 times per week or 2
  servings of white meat daily or for vegetarians,
  include at least 1–2 cups of dried peas and beans
  (e.g. lentils, soy beans, chick peas) daily   Yes/No
- I include a vitamin C source with meals
  based on bread, cereals, fruit and vegetables
  to assist the iron absorption in these
  'plant' sources of iron   Yes/No

Calcium checker

- I eat at least 3 serves of dairy food or soy milk alternative each day (1 serve = 200 ml milk or fortified soy milk; 1 slice (30 g) hard cheese; 200 g yoghurt) Yes/No

Fluids

- I drink fluids regularly before, during and after exercise Yes/No

Alcohol

- When I drink alcohol, I would mostly drink no more than is recommended for the safe drink driving limit Yes/No

(Cirle yes if you don't drink alcohol)

2. Score 1 point for every 'yes' answer

Scoring scale

18–20 Excellent	15–17 Room for improvement
12–14 Just made it	0–12 Poor

Note: Very active people will need to eat more breads, cereals and fruit than on this quiz, but to stay healthy no one should be eating less.

(Adapted from *The Taste of Fitness* by Helen O'Connor and Donna Hay)

SPORTS NUTRITION IN A NUTSHELL

High carbohydrate eating

To perform at its best, your body needs the right type of fuel. No matter what your sport, carbohydrates are the best fuel for you! High carbohydrate foods help enhance stamina and prevent fatigue. They include, breakfast cereals, bread, rice, pasta, fruit and vegetables (especially starchy vegetables like potato, corn and dried peas and beans). Sugars found in table sugar, honey, jam and confectionery are also useful sources of carbohydrate for active people.

Low fat eating

Fats are an essential part of your diet. A low to moderate fat intake helps active people maintain a lean physique. Eating the best types of fat and avoiding excessive fat intake is important for good health as well as best performance. The best types of fats for cooking include the mono-unsaturated fats like olive and canola oil and the polyunsaturated fats like sunflower and safflower oil. Watch out for the saturated fats found in many fast foods, butter, cream and the fat on meat.

Fat reducing strategies include:

- cutting the fat off meat (or using trim cuts)
- removing the skin from chicken
- using minimal amounts of fat in cooking
- using non-stick cookware

The amount of fat you need depends on your daily fuel requirements. For good health and weight maintenance we have included the following general guidelines. (5 g fat is equivalent to about 1 teaspoon mono- or polyunsaturated oil.)

Low fat diets	30–40 g fat per day
Most women and children	30–50 g fat per day
Most men	40–60 g fat per day
Teenagers and active adults	70 g fat per day
Larger and very active athletes/workers	80–100 g fat per day

Fat is an 'invisible' ingredient in many foods. Use a fat counter to help you identify some of the sources of fat in your diet. Keep a food record for a week and calculate your personal fat intake using the counter. It may surprise you! Comprehensive fat counters are readily available from bookshops and newsagents. We have also included a fat counter in the A–Z of Foods tables in this pocket guide starting on page 74.

ARE YOU REALLY CHOOSING LOW FAT?

There's a trick to food labels that it is worth being aware of when shopping for low fat foods. Nutrient claims are covered by food legislation that specifies what low fat really means.

Low fat means that the food must be 3% fat or less (3 g fat per 100 g food or 1.5 g fat per 100 g liquid food).

Reduced fat means that the food contains at least 25% less fat than the original food—in other words, no more than 75% of the fat found in the original food. A reduced fat food isn't low enough in fat to be called a low fat food.

A balanced diet
contains a wide
variety of low fat foods.

Don't forget protein

Athletes in heavy training have increased protein needs. Protein balance depends on the individual but you generally need at least 2 servings a day. Some athletes forget to include enough protein in their diet (2–3 serves per day). Body building athletes often consume protein in excess of their requirements. Good sources of protein include lean meat, poultry, fish and seafood, eggs, milk, cheese and yoghurt. Dried peas, beans and nuts are the best vegetable source. Bread and cereals provide smaller but still useful amounts of protein.

Fluids

The human body is 70 per cent water. During exercise you lose some of this water as sweat. If you don't replace it, you will become dehydrated and your body will overheat—like a car without water in its radiator.

- Small fluid losses decrease performance.
- Large fluid losses resulting in dehydration are life threatening!

During exercise, thirst is not a good indicator of your fluid needs. You usually need to drink more than your thirst dictates. Every kilogram lost during exercise approximates 1 litre of sweat losses to be replaced.

During exercise,
thirst is not a good indicator
of your fluid needs.

What to drink during exercise

Water is an adequate fluid replacer and is appropriate in many situations.

Sports and electrolyte drinks are absorbed into the bloodstream faster than water, replace carbohydrates and electrolytes and have a pleasant taste—which encourages greater fluid consumption. See 'The Case for High G.I. Foods' (pages 34–41) for more on sports drinks. The A–Z of Foods (page 91) gives the G.I. of sports drinks, such as Gatorade and Sports Plus. Please note that this does not refer to sport supplement drinks like Sustagen Sport, which is a liquid meal.

Soft drinks or fruit juice empty from the stomach slower than sports drinks or water and aren't suitable fluid replacers during exercise.

Note: The caffeine in cola-type soft drinks increases urine production and is dehydrating.

Adequate fluid replacement
during exercise enhances performance
and prevents heat stress.

Special nutrient considerations

Iron Iron deficiency is common in athletes, particularly female athletes, vegetarians, and those participating in strenuous training programs, especially endurance athletes. Many athletes don't consume adequate iron in their daily diet and may include excess caffeine or tannin (in tea) that bind up iron and reduce its absorption. The best sources of iron are red meats, liver and kidney. Plant sources contain lower amounts of iron which is not absorbed as well.

SOURCES OF IRON

(ranked from best to least):

★★★★ Red meats, liver, kidney

★★★ White meats and seafood

★★ Dried peas and beans
(baked beans, soy beans)

★ Bread, cereals and some vegetables

Did you know?

Including vitamin C rich fruits and vegetables in a meal improves the absorption or iron from plant sources (e.g. bread, cereals, vegetables, fruit).

Calcium Calcium is important for bone development in the young and for bone maintenance in adults. An adequate calcium intake and weight-bearing exercise throughout life is essential to build and then maintain optimal bone strength for both males and females.

Calcium is important
for bone development in the young
and for bone maintenance in adults.

In females, regular strenuous exercise, usually accompanied by factors such as fat loss, strict dieting or stress, can precipitate menstrual cycle interruptions. An irregular or absent menstrual cycle may result in a reduced level of the hormone oestrogen which is vital for maintaining calcium levels in bone and for enhancing calcium absorption from the diet. Menstrual irregularities of greater than six months need medical investigation. Athletes with very infrequent or absent menstrual cycles should have extra calcium in the range of 1000 to 1500 mg a day. This won't prevent bone loss but may help to slow down the rate of loss.

Nutritional supplements

Big dollars are spent promoting nutritional supplements for active people and athletes. Watch out for supplements with no scientific basis to the claims. If in doubt, ask a sports dietitian for help. Some supplements are beneficial in certain circumstances.

Supplements of iron or calcium may be required if inadequate amounts are consumed in the diet or if deficiency exists.

Supplements like sports drinks, liquid meals and carbohydrate loaders are also beneficial, not because they provide something magical but because they package energy and carbohydrate in a convenient and easy to consume form. This is especially useful to athletes who need an easily digested fuel on the run.

Sports bars and carbohydrate gels (available in sports and bike shops) are in a similar category to sports drinks etc.

Herbal supplements, amino acids and fat burners Unfortunately, solid evidence for these supplements is lacking. In many cases, scientific studies have shown absolutely nil effect.

Competition eating

Eating for competing is discussed in detail later in this book. Look under the following topics:

- pre-competition meal guidelines (page 44)
- the case for low G.I. foods (page 46)
- glycogen loading (page 42)
- recovery after exercise (page 34)
- the case for high G.I. foods (page 34)
- refuelling during an event (page 38)

If you want to find out about eating for competing in greater depth, take a look at one of the books on sports nutrition in the references on page 95 or consult a sports dietitian.

Whether you are one of the elite
or a weekend warrior,
the right diet can give you
the winning edge.

ENERGY CHARGE YOUR BODY WITH CARBOHYDRATE

Carbohydrate circulates in your body as glucose in the blood (blood sugar) and is stored as glycogen in the liver and muscles. When glycogen stores are depleted, fatigue sets in and performance suffers. Your body uses glucose to fuel movement and activity. Just as high speed cars require regular top-ups of petrol, active bodies need a regular supply of carbohydrate to top up glycogen stores.

Carbohydrate is the human body's favourite energy source for physical activity, especially high intensity exercise. But your body's carbohydrate stores are small, and need regular replenishing, generally every 4 to 5 hours.

Athletes feel tired and lethargic when they don't consume enough carbohydrate for their daily needs. When this happens and the glycogen in the muscles is depleted, fatigue sets in. That's when your muscles feel heavy and your pace slows. 'Hitting the wall', an expression used by endurance athletes, describes the feeling when glycogen stores are almost exhausted.

Active bodies need a regular supply of carbohydrate to top up on their glycogen stores.

Low blood sugar or 'hypoglycaemia'

Exercisers can also experience a type of fatigue related to the carbohydrate levels in their blood. It is possible for your muscle glycogen levels to be adequate while the blood sugar levels controlled by the liver, fall. Low blood sugar or 'hypoglycaemia' (cyclists call this 'bonking') occurs when you exercise in the morning before eating, or exercise hard after skipping a meal.

> *To maintain energy levels,*
> *athletes must consume enough carbohydrate*
> *to keep pace with their muscle glycogen needs*
> *and keep up a regular intake of carbohydrate*
> *to maintain blood sugar levels.*

Early morning exercise

If you exercise strenuously early in the morning, it's a good idea to have some carbohydrate before training or take some with you to have on the run! Most people have enough liver glycogen to fuel low intensity, short duration (<1 hour) exercise sessions. If you simply want to delay eating until after your light early morning walk, it's not a problem. However, eating before and/or during a strenuous cycling session makes good sense!

3 EASY STEPS TO ESTIMATE YOUR DAILY CARBOHYDRATE NEEDS

It is difficult to put an exact figure on anyone's carbohydrate needs. Use the table opposite as a rough guide and ask a sports dietitian for help if you are unsure.

Step 1. Weigh yourself naked or in minimal clothing in kilograms (no shoes or belts with heavy buckles!).

Step 2. Multiply your body weight by your activity level factor (see table opposite). This total gives you the **target carbohydrate intake in grams** that you must consume each day to meet your carbohydrate needs.

Step 3. Keep a food record for a few days and calculate your carbohydrate intake with a carbohydrate counter such as the one at the end of this book. Compare your actual carbohydrate intake with the target value you calculated. If it is way below the carbohydrate target, you have some serious carb eating to do! If you are within 50 g or even a little over your carbohydrate target that's fine! Use the carbohydrate counter to help you plan a higher carb intake.

Remember, this is a rough estimate.
You may need a little more or less.
See how you feel.

WHAT'S YOUR ACTIVITY LEVEL?

The amount of carbohydrate you need depends on your weight and activity level.

Activity level	Grams of carbohydrate per kg body weight per day
Light—Walking, light/easy swimming or cycling low impact/easy beat aerobic dance	4–5
Less than 1 hour per day	
Light-moderate—intermediate aerobic dance class, easy jog, non-competitive tennis (3 sets), netball	5–6
1 hour per day	
Moderate—1 hour run, serious training for recreational/competition sports such as soccer, basketball, squash	6–7
1–2 hours per day	
Moderate-heavy—most professional/elite training for competitive sport such as swimming, tennis, football, distance running (<marathon)	7–8
2–4 hours per day	
Heavy—Training for ironman events marathon running/swimming, Olympic distance triathlon	8–10
More than 4 hours per day	

- Activity levels refer to the intensity as well as the duration of the activity.
- Time refers to the amount of time you are physically active during training, not the amount of time at training.
- Body weight refers to ideal or 'healthy' body weight.

Step 1. Weight 58 kg

Step 2. Activity Moderate level (training for mid-distance fun runs such as City to Surf—recreational level)

Requires 6–7 g of carbohydrate per kilogram per day

Target carbohydrate level is

$6 \times 58 = 348$ g per day to $7 \times 58 = 406$ g per day

348–406 g per day

Step 3. Food record

JESSICA'S FOOD RECORD

Meal	Carbohydrate count (g)
Breakfast	
I cup of bran cereal	35
1/2 cup of milk	5
I slice of white toast with butter	15
150 ml no added sugar fruit juice	15
Snack	
I banana	32
Lunch	
I cheese and tomato sandwich on white bread	32
I low fat fruit yoghurt	26
I glass water	0

Snack

2 cracker biscuits with Vegemite™	12
I orange	10

Dinner

I small piece of steak	0
I medium potato	16
1/2 cup of mixed vegetables	7
2 small scoops reduced fat ice-cream	13

Supper

3 plain coffee biscuits	14

Total carbohydrate	**225**

Jessica's carbohydrate count is way below target.

To boost Jessica's carbohydrate intake, add:

I extra piece of toast at breakfast	15
I extra sandwich and fruit or juice at lunch	45
I cup cooked pasta or rice with dinner	55
I bread roll with dinner	30
I glass of hot milk at supper	7

Grand total boosted with the extra carbohydrate foods	**377 g**

This is in the middle of the recommended range for Jessica's weight and activity level. Depending on how she feels, slight adjustments may be required depending on variations in the intensity and duration of her training program.

WHICH CARBOHYDRATE FOODS ARE BEST?

Carbohydrate foods include breads, breakfast cereals, rice and pasta, fruit and vegetables, especially starchy vegetables like potato, corn and dried peas and beans. There are smaller amounts of carbohydrate in dairy foods and in processed foods containing sugars. The carbohydrate foods give you a range of nutrients essential for health. When you are establishing the overall balance of your diet it is important to consume more of the carbohydrate foods which contain a high proportion of nutrients rather than those without additional vitamins and minerals.

Many active people, especially athletes in heavy training who eat large volumes of food, easily meet their daily nutrient requirements. Their carbohydrate needs, however, are sometimes so high, they simply can't manage the volume they need to eat! Liquid meals or carbohydrate supplements can help these athletes with high energy requirements meet their energy needs in a less 'bulky' way.

Today, there's another vital consideration in selecting carbohydrate foods to boost your sports performance. It is the glycaemic index of a food—the G.I. factor.

WHAT IS THE G.I. FACTOR?

Research on the glycaemic index (what we call the G.I. factor) shows that different carbohydrate foods have dramatically different effects on blood sugar levels.

The G.I. factor ranks foods based on their immediate effect on your blood sugar levels.

The carbohydrate score board

The G.I. ranking of carbohydrate foods is similar to a point score ranking in sports performance. The fastest athlete scoring the most points goes to the top, the slowest scorer is ranked at the bottom. The G.I. ranks carbohydrate foods on the speed at which they enter the bloodstream. The faster a blood sugar response appears in the bloodstream after eating a food, the higher its ranking or its G.I. The longer it takes to observe a blood sugar response, the lower the G.I.

At the 'back of the pack' of carbohydrate foods are legumes e.g. soy beans, baked beans, lentils etc. These enter the bloodstream slowly and have a very low G.I. (soy beans have a G.I. between 14–18).

UNDERSTANDING THE G.I. FACTOR

The glycaemic index concept was first developed by Dr David Jenkins, a professor of nutrition at the University of Toronto, Canada, to help determine which foods were best for people with diabetes. Since then, scientists around the world, including three of the authors of this book, have tested the effect of many foods on blood sugar levels and clearly demonstrated the value of the glycaemic index.

The key is the rate of digestion

Carbohydrate foods that break down quickly during digestion have the highest G.I. factors. Conversely, carbohydrates which break down slowly, releasing glucose gradually into the bloodstream have low G.I. factors.

Low G.I.	**less than 55**
Intermediate G.I.	**55 to 70**
High G.I.	**more than 70**

HOW THE G.I. IS MEASURED?

You can't predict the G.I. of a food from its composition. To test the G.I., you need real people and real foods. Standardised methods are always followed so that scientists around the world can duplicate the tests and the results from one group of people can be directly compared with those from another. The glycaemic response to a test food is determined by measuring the rise in blood sugar level and monitoring how long this level stays elevated.

Pure glucose produces the greatest rise in blood sugar levels. All other foods have less effect when fed in equal amounts of carbohydrate. The G.I. of pure glucose is set at 100 and every other food is ranked on a scale from 0 to 100 according to its actual effect on blood sugar levels.

You can't predict the G.I. of a food
from its composition

1. To find out the G.I. of a food, a volunteer eats an amount of that food containing 50 g of carbohydrate (calculated from food composition tables)—50 g of carbohydrate is equivalent to 3 tablespoons of pure glucose powder.

2. Over the next 2 hours (3 hours if the volunteer has diabetes), a blood sample is taken every 15 minutes during the first hour and every 30 minutes thereafter and the blood sugar level of these samples is measured and recorded.

3. The blood sugar level is plotted on a graph and the area under the curve is calculated using a computer program (see Figure 1).

4. The volunteer's response to the test food is compared with his or her blood sugar response to 50 g of pure glucose (the reference food).

5. The reference food is tested on 2 or 3 separate occasions and an average value is calculated to reduce the effect of day-to-day variation in blood sugar responses.

Note: The G.I. factor of the test food is the average value of a group of 8 to 12 volunteers.

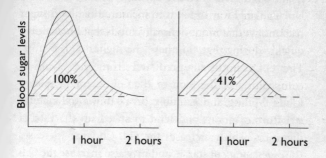

GLUCOSE (reference food)   SPAGHETTI (test food)

Blood sugar levels

100%   41%

1 hour   2 hours   1 hour   2 hours

Figure 1. The effect of a food on blood sugar levels is calculated using the area under the curve (hatched area). The area under the curve after consumption of the test food is compared with the same area after the reference food (usually 50 g of pure glucose or a 50 g carbohydrate portion of white bread).

Take some time to browse through the G.I. tables at the back of this book. Some of the G.I. factors may surprise you! At first it is hard to believe that sugar-containing foods may have a lower G.I. to fibrous, starchy foods like potato. But remember, these blood sugar responses have been measured numerous times and the tests have been repeated by different scientists around the world.

IS THERE AN EASY WAY TO TELL
IF A FOOD HAS A HIGH OR LOW G.I.?

No! The only way to tell is to measure the blood sugar response to that food. Generally, foods that break down quickly during digestion have the highest G.I. factors. The G.I. cannot be predicted from the chemical composition of the food or the G.I. factor of related foods. Milling and grinding break down the cellular structure of grains and tend to speed up the rate of digestion, which increases the G.I. Cooking increases the digestibility of starch, and may also increase the G.I. It might seem surprising but removing the dietary fibre in bread, rice or pasta has little effect on the G.I. However, the viscous fibre found in fruits and some grains (e.g. oats and barley) may account for their lower G.I. Fat slows the digestion process and lowers the G.I. in some instances.

The only way to tell if a food
has a high or low G.I.
is to measure it.

TRICKY TWINS

Circle the food in each of the following pairs which you think will have the lower G.I. factor.

Rice	Rice bubbles
Sweet corn	Cornflakes
Baked potatoes	French fries
Toasted muesli	Untoasted muesli
Grainy bread	Wholemeal bread

(Answers: Rice, Sweet corn, Baked potatoes, Toasted muesli, Grainy bread—depending on the brand.)

HOW CAN I CALCULATE THE G.I. OF A MIXED MEAL?

You calculate the G.I. of a mixed meal by averaging the G.I. of the different carbohydrate foods in the meal. Supposing you have baked beans on toast.

Regular white bread has a G.I. of 70 and baked beans have a G.I. of 48. If equal amounts of carbohydrate come from the baked beans and the bread then you add the G.I. factors and divide by two, e.g. (70 + 48)/2 = 59.

Say the meal contained one-quarter of the carbohydrate from baked beans to three-quarters of the carbohydrate from bread then 25 per cent of the G.I. factor for baked beans would be added to 75 per cent of the G.I. for bread. The following calculation shows how this is done.

$$
\begin{aligned}
\text{25 per cent of 48} &= 12 \\
\text{75 per cent of 70} &= 52.5 \\
\text{G.I. factor} &= 12 + 52.5 = 64.5
\end{aligned}
$$

But you really don't need to do calculations. All you need to remember is:

Low G.I. + High G.I. = Intermediate G.I.

HOW CAN I USE THE G.I. TO BOOST SPORTS PERFORMANCE?

There are several applications of the G.I. to sports performance. Sometimes it will be best for you to choose a high G.I. food, other times, a low G.I. food may be beneficial.

To date, most work on the G.I. factor and sports performance has concentrated on competition eating and recovery. Researchers are investigating other applications, especially the G.I. at each meal over the day when athletes are undergoing different training programs and exercise intensities. Scientific research has so far identified three key applications of the G.I. to enhance performance.

1. High G.I. foods in the recovery phase after exercise to accelerate glycogen replenishment.
2. High G.I. foods or fluids during exercise to maintain blood sugar levels.
3. A low G.I. pre-event meal may enhance endurance in prolonged exercise.

THE CASE FOR HIGH G.I. FOODS

RECOVERY AFTER EXERCISE

After exercise, your muscles are hungry for carbo-hydrate. Postponing carbohydrate consumption after exercise delays muscle glycogen replenishment and can cause fatigue.

- If you are a recreational exerciser, an adequate carbohydrate intake over the next few days will ensure that muscles are ready for another session.
- If you are participating in strenuous training, particularly when two or more training sessions are part of the daily routine, rapid glycogen replenishment is vital . Eat or drink carbohydrate (within 30 minutes) after strenuous exercise when another training session is on the agenda a few hours later. On consecutive days of competition, this recovery strategy will also assist in restocking your glycogen stores for the next event.

In the immediate post exercise period, high G.I. carbohydrates are best because they are digested and absorbed much faster and stimulate more insulin—the hormone responsible for getting glucose into the muscle and storing it as glycogen. Most athletes prefer high carbohydrate drinks because they are usually thirsty rather than hungry after strenuous exercise. A drink also aids rehydration.

Sports or electrolyte replacement drinks are ideal for replacing fluids and providing an immediate and convenient source of high G.I. carbohydrate.

After this initial 'hit' of recovery carbs, try to make sure your next meal or snack (within 2 hours) includes intermediate to high G.I. foods.

Recovery formula

The amount of carbohydrate required to kick off the recovery process is about 1 g per kilogram of body weight. Most people need between 50 to 100 grams of carbohydrate in the immediate post exercise period. Table 1 outlines a list of convenient high G.I. foods and sports drinks, suitable for recovery.

Postponing carbohydrate consumption after exercise delays muscle glycogen replenishment and can cause fatigue.

TABLE 1: SERVING SIZES OF HIGH G.I. FOODS TO ENHANCE RECOVERY

Food	G.I.	Serving size = 50 grams carbohydrate	Serving size = 75 grams carbohydrate
White or brown bread	70	100 grams (3 slices)	150 grams (4–5 slices)
Rice bubbles (Kelloggs)	89	45 grams (1 1/2 cups + 175 ml milk)	65 grams (2 cups + 300 ml milk)
Cornflakes (Kelloggs)	84	45 grams (1 1/2 cups + 175 ml milk)	65 grams (2 cups + 300 ml milk)
Scones	70	150 grams (2 large scones)	200 grams (3 large scones)
Morning coffee biscuits	79	65 grams (10 biscuits)	100 grams (15 biscuits)
Rice cakes	82	60 grams (5 rice cakes)	90 grams (8 rice cakes)
Muffins (English-style, toasted)	70	120 grams (2 muffins)	180 grams (3 muffins)
Rice (Calrose), cooked	83	180 grams (1 cup)	270 grams (1 1/2 cups)

Food	G.I.	Serving size = 50 grams carbohydrate	Serving size = 75 grams carbohydrate
Jelly beans	80	54 grams (6 jelly beans)	81 grams (9 jelly beans)
Sports electrolyte drink 6% carb	73–78	850 ml	1250 ml

Females weighing about 50 kilograms should aim to eat 50 grams of carbohydrate.

Males weighing about 75 kilograms should aim to eat 75 grams of carbohydrate.

DURING AN EVENT

High G.I. carbohydrate is the best choice to optimise performance as the carbohydrate needs to be rapidly available to the muscle as a fuel source. Consuming carbohydrate 'on the run' has been shown to delay fatigue as it provides energy to working muscles when the body's own stores of glycogen are low. This is especially the case when exercise is prolonged and even glycogen loading cannot prepare the body for the carbohydrate needed to get through the long endurance event.

If you don't have sufficient carbohydrate in your training diet, supplementing carbohydrate during exercise helps you keep pace when your glycogen stores are low. This is not a quick fix to avoid a high carbohydrate training diet! The body prefers to obtain carbs from glycogen stored in the muscle during exercise. Outside carbs are a great back up, but it's essential to prepare your body by eating a high carb training diet each day.

Table 2 lists high G.I. carbohydrates that are popular during exercise. Sports electrolyte replacement drinks are usually tolerated better because they are emptied more quickly from the stomach.

TABLE 2: HIGH G.I. CHOICES SUITABLE DURING EXERCISE

Food	G.I.	Serving size	Carbohydrate (g)
Sport drink (electrolyte)	73-78	1 litre	60-80
White bread with honey	70	2 slices with 2 tsp honey	40
Breakfast bar (fruit flavour)	78	1 bar	29
Jelly beans	80	100 g	60
Rice cakes	82	5 cakes	50
Scones	70	2 large	50

Prolong your endurance by topping up fluids and carbohydrate regularly throughout exercise.

Sports or electrolyte replacement drinks are ideal as they encourage greater fluid consumption than water, enhance intestinal absorption of fluid and provide carbohydrate while rehydrating the body at the same time. They are also less likely to cause gastrointestinal distress than solid foods. Getting the tummy wobbles during competition is not desirable!

The choice of solid or liquid carbohydrate during exercise is ultimately up to the individual, however, with the current sports/electrolyte formulations providing an optimal quickly absorbed source of carbs, it is hard to look past this as a primary option. Many exercisers choose a combination of sports drinks and comfortable solid foods they have trialled in training. Solids help in prolonged exercise to fill that 'empty' feeling in the stomach.

Many of the popular foods used during exercise over the years were adopted because they were convenient or easy to eat, rather than because they had a high G.I. The ever popular banana for example has an intermediate G.I. Eating a banana during exercise is not wrong. However, when the pace is really on and you want a fast energy supply, a more rapidly absorbing high G.I. option would technically be better. In prolonged exercise, you should aim to consume 30–60 g of carbohydrate per hour over the session (or event).

In long events, a combination of comfortable foods whatever their G.I. along with the high G.I. options will provide the best variety and feeling of psychological well being. The occasional mini chocolate bar as a treat may not scientifically be the best, highest G.I. fuel during exercise, but in the final stages of the ironman, it may boost your morale enough to keep you going. These psychological factors cannot be underestimated.

Use this book as a guide then start experimenting with different foods and fluids throughout training sessions. Discover for yourself what feels most comfortable and works best for you.

EATING FOR COMPETING: CARBOHYDRATE LOADING—WHAT A LOAD OF GLYCOGEN!

Carbohydrate (or glycogen) loading increases the body's store of glycogen in the liver and muscles. The extra glycogen provides additional fuel for endurance exercise where a normal glycogen store will not be sufficient to maintain stamina.

Early loading methods included a glycogen depletion phase which was employed to make the muscles 'hungry' for glycogen. These early regimes were like torture as athletes felt tired, irritable and had difficulty maintaining motivation and concentration. After 2–3 days of the depletion phase a high carbohydrate diet providing 9–10 g of carbohydrate for every kilogram of body weight was consumed for a further 3 days. During this time glycogen stores increased by 200–300 per cent.

In recent times, a modified carbohydrate loading regimen has been developed that results in a similar glycogen store without the unpleasant 'depletion' phase. Athletes simply taper training in the week prior to competition and consume a high carbohydrate diet as described above for 2–3 days prior to competition.

DO YOU NEED TO CARBOHYDRATE LOAD?

All athletes need an adequate normal store of carbohydrate to maximise performance. Carbohydrate loading, in its true sense, is only needed for endurance athletes exercising for greater than 120 minutes in duration e.g. those competing in sports like triathlon, marathon running or ironman events.

WHAT ABOUT THE G.I. AND CARBOHYDRATE LOADING?

At present there is insufficient scientific evidence to recommend a particular G.I. for carbohydrate loading. It appears that high G.I. diets may result in higher muscle glycogen levels in non athletes. It would seem reasonable to propose that a higher G.I. diet may facilitate more effective glycogen loading, but further research is needed.

*Carbohydrate loading increases
the body's store of glycogen.
This helps prevent fatigue
in endurance events.*

THE PRE-COMPETITION MEAL

The pre-competition meal has the potential to either make or break your performance on the day. What you eat should not be left to chance. Work on a dietary strategy using the following guidelines, then practise this strategy before a training session so you can fine tune your pre-competition meal.

Guidelines

- Eat 2–4 hours before the event. This allows time for your pre-competition meal to be emptied from the stomach. Allow 4 hours for a larger meal.
- Make the meal high in carbohydrate for maximum energy.
- Top up, do not over eat. Eat a comfortable amount of food.
- Keep the fat down in this meal. Fat slows digestion.
- Moderate protein. Fill up on carbohydrates instead.
- Moderate fibre. Too much high fibre food could cause bloating, diarrhoea and be uncomfortable during the competition.

- Drink your meal. If you're too nervous, or you feel it's too early in the morning to eat, try a sports drink or liquid meal type drink (e.g. Sustagen™) so that you can maintain your energy with liquid food.
- Practise. Experiment with different meals to find out what works best for you.

ON YOUR MARK
Remember, the pre-event meal won't work miracles if your training diet is inadequate. Make sure you are eating well generally, especially for the week leading up to competition.

GET SET
Use these pre-competition guidelines to help you plan your pre-event meal.

GO
During exercise, replace fluids and carbohydrates regularly as you go.

THE CASE FOR LOW G.I. FOODS

THE PRE-EVENT MEAL

Researchers at the University of Sydney have found that a low G.I. pre-event meal, at least 1 hour prior to endurance exercise, can delay fatigue by delivering greater amounts of carbohydrate to the muscle late in exercise. If you think about it, the low G.I. meal will still be digesting during the exercise session and providing an additional source of carbohydrate that you had long forgotten about. Slow-release (low G.I.) carbohydrate is thought to be particularly useful for exercise of long duration where glycogen stores become limiting.

Athletes like to eat foods that won't be too heavy or fibrous. Before the event, choose low G.I. foods that are not too fibrous or 'gas producing'—taking a 'pit stop' at the loo during exercise can be very inconvenient! Suitable light and low G.I. foods include pasta, some varieties of rice (Basmati, Doongara), low G.I. breads (those with barley or wholegrains) and some breakfast cereals (e.g. porridge).

If you participate in prolonged (>2 hours) exercise, try a low G.I. pre-event meal to see if this works for you.

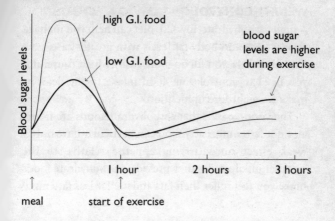

Comparison of the effect of low and high G.I. foods on blood sugar levels during prolonged strenuous exercise. When a pre-event meal of lentils (low G.I. factor) was compared with potatoes (high G.I. factor), cyclists were able to continue cycling at a high intensity (65 per cent of their peak aerobic capacity) for 20 minutes longer after eating the lentil meal. Their blood sugar and insulin levels were significantly higher at the end of exercise, indicating that carbohydrate was still being absorbed from the small intestine even after 90 minutes of strenuous exercise.

WEIGHT CONTROL

A high carbohydrate, low G.I. diet can help you manage your weight and body fat levels with greater ease. Low G.I. foods help you fill up more easily which is useful if you need to control your food intake to stay lean or make a weight for competition.

The good news is that carbohydrate foods are filling and not fattening. Fatty foods, in particular have only a weak effect on satisfying appetite relative to the number of kilojoules they provide. Carbohydrate foods make you feel fuller than fats and are far less fattening!

In studies at the University of Sydney, people were given a range of foods that contained equal numbers of kilojoules, then their satiety (feeling of fullness and satisfaction after eating) responses were compared. High carbohydrate, low G.I. foods were the most filling and satisfying.

If you need to increase your food intake to gain lean body mass, excessive amounts of low G.I. food may be just too filling. In this case, you need to balance the G.I. in your meals so you can consume enough food.

COUNTING THE KILOJOULES
IN OUR NUTRIENTS

All foods contain kilojoules. Of all the nutrients in food that we consume, fat yields the most kilojoules per gram.

carbohydrate	16 kilojoules per gram
protein	17 kilojoules per gram
alcohol	29 kilojoules per gram
fat	37 kilojoules per gram

*Low fat, low G.I.
carbohydrate foods help
you to feel full and
more satisfied after eating.*

DID YOU KNOW?

1 calorie = 4.2 kilojoules

THE CASE STUDIES

The following case studies will help you understand the principles of sports nutrition in action. Each case presents common problems or questions and provides simple, practical solutions.

Use this book and others recommended on page 95 to help you plan a better diet to boost your own sports performance. If you get stuck, don't be afraid to seek professional help from a dietitian who is trained to plan out a diet for your specific needs.

Remember, these cases are to be used as a guide only. It is best if you can use the general principles to discover what works best for you.

GO FOR IT!

NATHAN—AUSTRALIAN RULES FOOTBALL

Nathan is an 18-year-old Australian Rules football player. He recently moved from a small country town to take up a position in one of the best sides in the league. Playing professional footy was Nathan's dream. Wanting to make a big impression during his first few weeks at training, Nathan gave his all. At first he felt fine, but after one week of training twice almost every day he felt exhausted, and was frankly 'off the pace'. Sensing that Nathan was struggling, the coach took him aside and recommended he speak to the club's sports dietitian about his diet and recovery strategies.

Nathan's Weekly Training Program

Morning weight/circuit training:
2–3 sessions per week of 1–1.5 hours
Afternoon football/fitness sessions:
4 sessions of 2–2.5 hours per week

Consultation with the sports dietitian

Nathan was a bit wary, he wondered what diet could really do for him. The dietitian explained that carbohydrates were the key to energy and recovery. His diet at the moment was far too low in carbohydrate to get him through the tough pre-season training. The dietitian also explained that eating carbohydrate regularly was important, and fuelling up immediately (within 30 minutes) after training sessions helped to replace the body's carbohydrate stores more quickly. Timing was important because between morning and afternoon training his body had less than 6 hours to refuel. More rapidly absorbing carbs or those with an intermediate to high G.I. were also better for refuelling as they replenished the body's carbohydrate or glycogen levels faster.

The dietitan also explained that to help Nathan maintain his body weight and stay lean he should:

- use lean meats or cut off the fat
- remove chicken skin from chicken
- use reduced fat dairy products
- minimise use of oils, butter or margarine

High G.I. fuel to the rescue

Nathan noticed the other players were already doing this. They consumed sports drinks with glucose (high G.I.) to begin the refuelling and rehydration process straight after training and chose intermediate to high G.I. breads, cereals or fruit to boost their recovery (French bread, Weet-Bix™, Wheatbites™, Breakfast Bar™, pineapple, watermelon). These foods were available at training so he could start the refuelling process before travelling home.

The dietitian also organised cooking classes to give him confidence preparing different carbohydrate-based meals for himself. But Nathan now knew that when recovery time was short, higher G.I. carbohydrate meals were best.

Results

Nathan noticed the difference in his performance after being on the high carbohydrate diet for only a few days. He felt fresher at afternoon training and could really power through the sprint sessions which had been like torture before. Including more carbohydrate in his diet and refuelling with higher G.I. carbohydrates really helped him. He knew he still had a lot of work to do before the competition season kicked off but with the right fuel, a great attitude and some raw talent he reckoned he was ready for some of his best ever performances.

MEAL PLAN FOR NATHAN

Aim: To provide sufficient carbohydrate and energy and to assist recovery rate by incorporating high G.I. liquids and intermediate-to-high G.I. meals after training.

8.30 am Immediately post training
1 litre sports/electrolyte drink

Post training

9.00 am Breakfast:

Intermediate to high G.I. choices

1 piece of fruit — Pineapple, Watermelon
2 cups of cereal — Puffed wheat, Weet-bix, Wheatbites

2 cups of reduced fat milk
2 slices white or wholemeal toast (no butter) — White or wholemeal with a high G.I. (see tables)
with honey — French bread has a high G.I.
1 glass of fruit juice — Pineapple is his favourite juice

11.30 am Snack
1 sandwich (no butter) lean meat filling
1 piece of fruit (any type)
1 low fat yoghurt

1.00 pm Lunch
3 salad sandwiches or rolls filled with any of the following: lean meat, chicken reduced fat cheese, egg, canned tuna in spring water or canned salmon
2 pieces of fresh fruit (any type)
600 ml of reduced fat, flavoured milk

2.30 pm Snack

Fruit smoothie or a liquid meal
(e.g. Sustagen™)

**Intermediate to high
G.I. choices**

....

3.30-5.30 pm Pre- and during training

2–3 litres of sports/electrolyte drink   High G.I. (73–78)

....

5.30 pm After training:

1 litre sports/electrolyte drink or
carb loader   High G.I. for recovery

....

7 pm. Dinner

Large serving lean meat (155 g),
or skinless chicken (185 g), or
fish (250 g)—grilled or cooked
with minimum oil

Large serving of rice, or pasta or   High G.I. rice on training
potato   nights, pasta most others

Medium serving of vegetables or
tossed green salad (no-oil dressing)

4 slices of white bread or 2 rolls   High G.I. French bread
(no butter)   on training nights

....

9.00 pm Snack

2 pieces of fresh fruit in a smoothie
or fruit and yoghurt

Dietary analysis

Energy:	18 821 kilojoules (4480 Calories)
Protein:	194 g (17 per cent)
Fat:	67 g (14 per cent)
Carbohydrate:	775 g (69 per cent)

ANALISE—BALLET DANCER

Analise, a 16-year-old full-time ballet student, had a dream: to be a dancer with the Australian Ballet Company. When she started to mature at 13, she found she could no longer 'eat anything' as she used to. Extra weight started to pile on. First she tried all the diets given to her by the other ballet students, but she always felt hungry and craved chocolate. Getting nowhere fast by herself, her mother took her to see a sports dietitian.

Consultation with the sports dietitian

At their first meeting the dietitian took a history of Analise's weight and eating patterns and found that a typical day's meals for Analise included:

A slice of white toast with butter and a cup of strong black tea for breakfast

2 crispbreads with butter and a cup of black tea for a morning snack

A green salad, an apple and a cup of black tea for lunch

A chocolate bar and a can of diet cola during the afternoon (waiting at the train station)

Steamed vegies, sometimes steamed chicken and a cup of black tea for dinner

A chocolate bar or chocolate biscuits and tea for supper.

The dietitian explained that this diet was high in fat and too low in protein, carbohydrate, calcium and iron. She explained that:

- Gaining a little body weight and fat is part of the maturation process and that the best way to control body fat was with a sensible diet, not starving.
- Cravings are to be expected when you are hungry. After working hard in class all day with virtually no food, chocolate is just too tempting. Eating more carbohydrate on a regular basis would help Analise control her chocolate cravings.
- Analise needed a dietary strategy to give her sufficient fuel to get through the day without feeling hungry. Carbohydrates (especially carbs with a low G.I.) would help her to feel fuller (satiety), give her more energy and are much less fattening than fats. Analise's meal plan, based on reducing fat intake and boosting carbohydrate, meant eating more pasta, rice, bread, fruit and vegetables and less high fat food like butter and chocolate. Chocolate was not totally out but she had to cut back to get her body fat levels going in the right direction. The dietitian also explained that reducing the cups of tea would help Analise maintain adequate iron levels. The tannin in tea reduces iron absorption.

Analise had some questions about the meal plan.

Could she really lose weight eating this much?
The dietitian explained that the size or appearance of foods is often deceiving. Although some high fat foods like chocolate look compact, and foods like bread and vegetables may take up more space on the plate, the fat and kilojoule (calorie) value of high fat foods is much more than bread and vegetables. The fat figures in the back of this book were a real surprise to Analise as was the fact that the fat we eat is converted into body fat, faster and easier than anything else we eat.

Should she cut out chocolate all together?
The dietitian explained that giving up chocolate is really not necessary and is almost impossible unless you live somewhere where there's no chocolate at all. Eating chocolate as a treat rather than a substitute meal is the key.

How could she avoid feeling too full and having a bloated stomach during class?

Foods with a high fibre content (including many salad vegies) produce more gas in the intestine and this can cause bloating. The dietitian showed how Analise could increase the intake of low G.I. carbs through the day without bloating.

Results

At first Analise kept thinking that she was eating too much. But she found avoiding the chocolate vending machine on the station platform on the way home easier when she felt fuller through the day, the high carb, low G.I. foods really reduced her hunger. Her body fat level (measured with body fat or skinfold callipers) dropped steadily each week. It was almost unbelievable to be able to drop fat without starving. An added bonus was her improved energy levels and concentration in class, not to mention her mood which was more relaxed and cheerful.

ANALISE'S MEAL PLAN

Aim: To provide a regular supply of carbohydrate, with less fat. The G.I. to be intermediate to low to assist with satiety.

8.00 am Breakfast	**Intermediate to low G.I.**
1 piece of fruit	Fresh apple, grapefruit, kiwi fruit
1 cup bran type cereal	All Bran, oats, Sultana Bran™
1 slice wholegrain toast (no butter) and jam	Oat, barley, mixed grain or fruit breads
1 cup decaffeinated coffee	

....

10.30 am Snack	
1 piece of fruit or a low fat fruit yoghurt	Fruit like, apricot, cherries, orange

....

1.00 pm Lunch	
1 sandwich (no butter). Protein options include: chicken, turkey, canned tuna in brine or water, salmon, reduced fat cheese, lean ham, corn beef or roast meat.	Oat, barley or heavy grain bread
Small amount of salad	
1 piece of fruit	Peach, pear or plum
Water or a low joule drink (not containing caffeine)	

....

3.30 pm Snack	
1 raisin toast with jam or 1/2 English muffin with jam.	Raisin bread or grain muffin
Or fruit or low fat yoghurt as in morning snack	

....

7.00 pm Dinner

Small serving of lean meat (90 g),
or skinless chicken (125 g) or
grilled fish (155 g).
All cooked in minimum to no oil.
2 potatoes or pasta
or Basmati or Doongara rice
Large serving of vegetables
or salad with low oil dressing
Water or low joule cordial

Intermediate to low G.I.

New boiled potatoes, pasta
Basmati or Doongara rice

....

9.30 pm Supper

1 glass of reduced fat milk
1 slice raisin toast with jam

Dietary analysis

Energy:	5640 kilojoules (1300 Calories)
Protein:	80 g (24 per cent)
Fat:	20 g (14 per cent)
Carbohydrate:	208 g (62 per cent)
Calcium	800 mg (equal to the recommended daily intake)
Iron	14–18 mg (above the recommended daily intake)

IAN—IRONMAN TRIATHLETE

Ian is a 26-year-old physical education teacher and keen triathlete. He has competed in the Olympic distance for the past 5 years but is now keen to qualify for the ironman triathlon in Hawaii. Ian wanted everything to be spot on for his first ironman race so he could qualify for Hawaii. He approached a sports dietitian to help him plan his dietary strategy and brought a list of questions to ask.

How much carbohydrate does he need in his training diet?

The approximate amount of carbohydrate Ian needs is calculated by multiplying his weight by the carbohydrate requirement appropriate for his activity level

Ian's weight	75 kg
Approximate carbohydrate requirement for his activity level (see page 21)	8 g/kg
Daily carbohydrate needs for training	75 x 8 = 600 g

This amount of carbohydrate may be too difficult to achieve with food. Liquid carbohydrate supplements like sports drinks can help boost carbohydrate intake.

Ian's Training Program

	AM Training	PM Training
Monday	3 km swim	Track session + 15 km run
Tuesday	3 km swim	100 km cycle
Wednesday	Rest	15 km run
Thursday	3 km swim	100 km cycle
Friday	3 km swim	50 km easy cycle
Saturday	150 km cycle	3 km swim
Sunday	Rest	30 km run

Ian's Vital Statistics

Height 178 cm

Weight 75 kg (has lost 4 kg over the past 3 months)

Sum of 8 skinfolds 50 mm (indicates that Ian is very lean)

How can he incorporate the G.I. into his training diet? Ian can incorporate the G.I. in his diet mainly by including high G.I. drinks (e.g. sports drinks) during and after training. Intermediate to high G.I. foods after training also help to speed up recovery. At other times, the most important thing is to eat sufficient carbohydrate whatever the G.I. (Most athletes requiring the amount of carbohydrate that Ian does will feel more comfortable with moderate to lower fibre carbohydrate choices (e.g. white bread, white rice and pasta instead of the wholegrain varieties). Otherwise the sheer volume of the carbohydrate and fibre becomes too bulky and bloating.

Why was he so fatigued lately?
Fatigue is a generalised symptom that has numerous causes. Dietary factors that should be considered include:

- Low iron intake. If this is low, then increased amounts of high iron foods need to be included in the diet. Iron deficiency even in athletes with adequate iron intake does occur, and is more common in endurance athletes.
- Inadequate carbohydrate intake. Fatigue can be experienced if muscle glycogen stores are low indicating inadequate intake of carbohydrate over the day. Tiredness can also be due to low blood sugar. This may occur if there is a long period between meals. Low blood sugar (hypoglycaemia) commonly occurs in early morning or afternoon training sessions where insufficient carbohydrate is consumed before the session.

- Overtraining is a common problem with endurance athletes. Training programs need to be tailored to the individual, incorporating their personal needs for sleep and taking into account their occupational demands.

Viral illness and a number of other medical conditions are also potential causes of fatigue. Ian would benefit from a referral to a sports physician and an exercise scientist to investigate which factors in particular are causing his fatigue.

Does he need to glycogen load prior to the event?

Since the event will be longer than 2 hours (about 11 hours actually), yes! The meal plan outlines how he can glycogen load using the modified regimen. This regimen involves tapered training and a high carbohydrate diet 3–4 days prior to the race. The diet should provide about 9–10 g of carbohydrate per kg of body weight. Check the meal plan for guidance.

What would be the best pre-event meal?

Ian would benefit from trying a low G.I. meal in practice to see how this worked for him. To maintain gastric comfort, the best low G.I. options would include lower fibre choices such as, white pasta, rolled oats, or a liquid low fat milk based meal (Sustagen Sport™).

How could he maintain energy throughout the event?

During the event, maintaining energy and hydration will be a major factor influencing his performance. Sports drinks would be the best option to replace energy and fluids during the race. As sports drinks have a high G.I., they will be a rapidly absorbed and easily available source of carbohydrate. Other high G.I. options include carbohydrate gels, jelly beans, honey sandwiches on high G.I. (white French) bread. As Ian will only be able to carry a small amount of the high G.I. food options, the sports drink will probably provide the basis of his refuelling strategy with foods offering minor support.

To prevent boredom and as a morale booster some of the other offerings at the aid stations (choc chip cookie, jam sandwich, cola drink) could be included in smaller quantities as treats. These provide more of a psychological incentive than physiological boost. Although a little caffeine in the cola drink may help with fatigue later in the race due to its simulant properties. Ian needs to limit caffeine ingestion to avoid problems with its dehydration effect and slower stomach emptying which may compromise hydration. Caffeine is also subject to drug testing.

IAN'S MEAL PLAN

Aim: To provide sufficient carbohydrate and nutrition for peak performance. The meal plan should include intermediate to high G.I. meals or snacks after training sessions to help maximise the rate of glycogen replacement.

Regular training	Notes on G.I. Intermediate to high G.I. Post training	Loading phase
Breakfast		
1–2 pieces of fresh fruit	Pineapple, watermelon	Same breakfast
2 cups cereal	Weet-bix, Puffed Wheat,	
1 cup reduced fat milk	Wheatbites	
3 slices of toast with honey (no butter)	High G.I. bread	
500 ml fruit juice	Pineapple	
Snack		
1 banana and honey roll		As for training plan but add in an additional banana roll or a healthy fruit muffin
1 glass (250 ml) juice (any type)		
Lunch		
3 sandwiches with salad (including cheese, chicken, lean meat, egg, tuna or salmon as fillings)		Same lunch but add in a honey or jam sandwich for extra carbohydrate
1 piece fruit		
1 glass sports drink		
Snack		
As for morning tea or a fruit smoothie		Use a liquid meal e.g. Sustagen™ or carb loader. Ensure adequate fluid replacement
Before and during training Sports drink (volume dependent on session type and duration)		

Regular training	Notes on G.I. Intermediate to high G.I. Post training	Loading phas_
Dinner		
Medium serving of lean meat (125g), skinless chicken (155 g), fish (200 g) or a vegetarian meal		Same dinner
Large serving of potato, rice or pasta	High G.I. rice, great after hard afternoon training sessions	
Medium serving of vegetables or tossed green salad, no-oil dressing.		
4 slices of bread or two rolls	High G.I. bread	
2 pieces of fresh fruit	Pineapple, watermelon	
1 glass (250 ml) juice (any)		

....

Supper		
4 pieces raisin toast with jam or honey		Add in a carb-loader drink or a liquid meal e.g. Sustagen
1 glass fruit juice		

....

Dietary analysis (training)
Energy: 16 700 kilojoules
(3977 Calories)
Protein: 179 g (18 per cent)
Fat: 85 g (19 per cent)
Carbohydrate: 624 g (63 per cent)

Dietary analysis (loading)
Energy: 18 925 kilojoules
(4500 Calories)
Protein: 195 g (17 per cent)
Fat: 85 g (16 per cent)
Carbohydrate: 745 g
(67 per cent)

THE PRE-EVENT MEAL PLAN FOR IAN

This meal should be consumed about 2–3 hours prior to competition. Ian had tried out the low G.I. meal in training and wanted to use it in competition. The meals he found most comfortable included:

- Liquid meal (Sustagen Sport) plus a serving of stewed apple   G.I. = 39
- Rolled oats with skim milk and orange juice   G.I. = 44
- Tinned spaghetti on grain bread toast   G.I. = 47

Results

Ian went on to qualify for Hawaii. Being prepared for this race was crucial to best performance. The Hawaii Ironman was 'awesome'—one of his best-ever life experiences made more enjoyable by being well prepared and well fuelled.

YOUR G.I. QUESTIONS ANSWERED

What should be the overall G.I. of an athlete's diet?

This is a good question and one the scientists are yet to answer. There is evidence that diets with a higher G.I. increase the glycogen storage in the muscle of sedentary individuals. This may help athletes to store glycogen more effectively on a day to day basis. A high G.I. has been shown to enhance the rate of recovery of muscle glycogen after exercise. During exercise, a high G.I. is required to provide a rapidly available fuel source.

I am a recreational jogger, what should be the G.I. of my overall diet?

If the exercise is undertaken as part of a weight loss program, there may be some benefit in choosing low G.I. carbohydrates at each meal for their high satiety value. In general for recreational joggers, it is important to have sufficient carbohydrate in the diet for good health and energy. Since the time to restore glycogen after a work out is likely to be longer than for elite athletes, there is less need to have high G.I. carbohydrates immediately after exercise.

What about the pre-event meal before high intensity or non-endurance exercise?

As mentioned there is evidence that low G.I.

carbohydrates before endurance exercise may help to enhance performance. Studies on shorter term exercise have not been done so we again need to await further research. At this stage, there are many factors to consider in planning an optimal pre-event meal. The timing, the fibre content so as to prevent bloating, the fat content and of course the G.I. Much of the advice about pre-event eating has come from practical experience, and surprisingly little from scientific research. As so many factors need to be considered, the best advice for shorter term exercise at present is for individuals to consider the list of optimal pre-event eating strategies and experiment with foods or meals to determine what works best for them.

What about eating between heats and trials over the day?
There is insufficient scientific evidence to recommend a particular G.I. between events at present. However, it makes sense to include carbohydrates that are rapidly absorbed (i.e. higher G.I.) on a regular basis over the day. Eat little and often. Maintain fluid intake to optimise hydration. In shorter (<1 hour) breaks, rapidly absorbed liquids are probably best. In longer breaks, small low fat, high carb snacks (e.g. rice cakes, soft fruits, honey sandwiches, sports bars etc.) are recommended.

HOW TO USE THE G.I. TABLES

These simplified tables are an A to Z listing of the G.I. factor of foods commonly eaten in Australia and New Zealand. Approximately 300 different foods are listed. They include some new values for foods tested only recently.

The G.I. value shown next to each food is the average for that food using glucose as the standard, i.e., glucose has a G.I. value of 100, with other foods rated accordingly. The average may represent the mean of 10 studies of that food world wide or only 2 to 4 studies. In a few instances, Australian data are different to the rest of the world and we show our data rather than the average. Rice and porridge fall into this category.

We have included some foods in the list which are not commonly eaten (gram dahl) and other foods which may be encountered on overseas trips (processed breakfast cereals such as Rice Chex and Cheerios).

To check on a food's G.I., simply look for it by name in the alphabetic list. You may also find it under a food type—fruit, biscuits.

Included in the tables is the carbohydrate (CHO) and fat content of a sample serving of the food. This is to help you keep track of the amount of fat and carbohydrate in your diet. Refer to pages 18 and 10 for advice on how much carbohydrate and fat is recommended.

Remember when you are choosing foods, the G.I. factor isn't the only thing to consider. In terms of your blood sugar levels you should also consider the amount of carbohydrate you are eating. For your overall health the fat, fibre and micronutrient content of your diet is also important. A dietitian can guide you further with good food choices.

If you can't find a G.I. value for a food you eat on many occasions please write to us enclosing a stamped self-addressed envelope and we'll give you an estimated value of the food and endeavour to test its G.I. in the future. Address your letter to:

Associate Professor Jennie Brand Miller,
Human Nutrition Unit,
Department of Biochemistry,
University of Sydney, NSW 2006.
Fax 61 (02) 9351 6022
Email j.brandmiller@biochem.usyd.edu.au

A–Z OF FOODS
WITH G.I. FACTOR, CARBOHYDRATE & FAT

FOOD	GI	Fat	CHO
		(grams per serve)	
All Bran™, 1/3 cup, 40g	42(av)	1	22
Angel food cake, 30 g	67	trace	17
Apple, 1 medium, 150 g	38 (av)	0	18
Apple juice unsweetened, 1 cup, 250 ml	40	0	33
Apple muffin, 1 muffin, 80 g	44	9	44
Apricots, fresh, 3 medium, 100 g	57	0	7
canned, light syrup, 1/2 cup, 125 g	64	0	13
dried, 5-6 pieces, 30 g	31	0	13
Bagel, 1 white, 70 g	72	1	35
Baked beans, canned in tomato sauce, 1/2 cup, 120 g	48 (av)	1	13
Banana cake, 1 slice, 80 g	47	7	46
Banana, raw, 1 medium, 150 g	55 (av)	0	32
Barley, pearled, boiled, 1/2 cup, 80 g	25 (av)	1	17
Basmati white rice, boiled, 1 cup, 180 g	58	0	50
Beetroot, canned, drained, 2-3 slices, 60 g	64	0	5
Bengal gram dahl, 1/2 cup, 100 g	54	5	57
Biscuits			
Digestives plain, 2 biscuits, 30 g	59 (av)	6	21
Graham Wafers, 4 biscuits, 30 g	74	3	22

FOOD	GI	Fat	CHO
		(grams per serve)	
Biscuits *(continued)*			
Oatmeal, 2 biscuits, 20 g	55	3	15
Milk Arrowroot, 2 biscuits, 16 g	69	2	13
Morning Coffee, 3 biscuits, 18 g	79	2	14
Rich Tea, 2 biscuits, 20 g	55	3	16
Shredded Wheatmeal, 2 biscuits, 16 g	62	2	12
Shortbread, 2 biscuits, 30 g	64	8	19
Vanilla wafers, 6 biscuits, 30 g	77	5	21
see also Crackers			
Black bean soup, 220 ml	64	2	82
Black beans, boiled, 3/4 cup, 120 g	30	1	26
Black gram, soaked and boiled, 120 g	43	1	16
Blackbread, dark rye, 1 slice, 50 g	76	1	21
Blackeyed beans, soaked, boiled, 1/2 cup, 120 g	42	1	24
Blueberry muffin,1 muffin, 80 g	59	8	41
Bran			
Oat bran, 1 tablespoon, 10 g	55	1	7
Rice bran, extruded, 1 tablespoon, 10 g	19	2	3
Bran Buds ™, 1/3 cup, breakfast cereal, 30 g	58	1	14
with psyllium, 1/3 cup, 30 g	47	0	12
Bran muffin, 1, 80 g	60	8	34
Breads			
Burgen™ Oat Bran & Honey Loaf			
with Barley, 1 slice, 40 g	31	2	14

FOOD	GI	Fat	CHO
		(grams per serve)	
Breads *(continued)*			
Dark rye, Blackbread, 1 slice, 50 g	76	1	21
Dark rye, Schinkenbröt, 1 slice, 50 g	86	1	22
French baguette, 30 g	95	1	15
Fruit loaf, heavy, 1 slice, 35 g	47	1	18
Gluten free bread, 1 slice, 30 g	90	1	14
Hamburger bun, 1 prepacked bun, 50 g	61	3	24
Kaiser roll, 1 roll, 50 g	73	1	25
Light rye, 1 slice, 50 g	68	1	23
Linseed rye, 1 slice, 50 g	55	5	21
Melba toast, 4 squares, 30 g	70	1	19
Pita bread, 1 piece, 65 g	57	1	38
Ploughman's Loaf™ mixed grain, 1 slice, 45 g	47	1	21
Pumpernickel, 1 slice, 60 g	41	1	21
Riga Sunflower & Barley, 1 slice, 40 g	57	1	17
Rye bread, 1 slice, 50 g	65	1	23
Sourdough rye, 1 slice, 50 g	57	2	23
Vogel's™ Honey & Oat loaf 1 slice, 40 g	55	3	17
Vogel's™ Roggenbrot™, 1 slice, 35-40 g	59	1	18
White (wheat flour), 1 slice, 30 g	70 (av)	1	15
Wholemeal (wheat flour), 1 slice, 35 g	69 (av)	1	14
Wonderwhite™(with Hi-Maize™), 1 slice, 35 g	80	1	17
Bread stuffing, 60 g	74	5	17
Breadfruit, 120 g	68	1	17

FOOD	GI	Fat	CHO
		(grams per serve)	
Breakfast cereals			
All-Bran™, 1/3 cup, 40 g	42 (av)	1	22
Bran			
Oat bran, 2 tablespoons, 10 g	55	1	7
Rice bran, extruded, 1 tablespoon, 10 g	19	2	3
Corn bran breakfast cereal, 1/2 cup, 30 g	75	1	20
Bran Buds ™, 1/3 cup, 30 g	58	1	14
with psyllium, 1/3 cup, 30 g	47	0	12
Breakfast Bar, Fibre Plus, Uncle Tobys,			
1 bar, 42.5 g	78	4	29
Cheerios ™, 30 g	74	2	20
Cocopops™, 3/4 cup, 30 g	77	0	26
Corn Chex , 30 g	83	0	25
Cornflakes, 1 cup, 30 g	84 (av)	0	26
Crispix, 30 g	87	1	26
Mini Wheats™ (whole wheat), 1 cup, 30 g	58	0	21
Muesli, toasted, 1/2 cup, 60 g	43	10	33
Muesli, non-toasted, 1/2 cup, 60 g	56	6	32
Nutri-grain™, 1 cup, 30 g	66	0	20
Oat bran, raw, 1 tablespoon, 10 g	55	1	7
Porridge (cooked with water) 1/2 cup, 130 g	46 (av)	1	12
Puffed wheat,1 cup, 30 g	80	1	22
Rice bran, 1 tablespoon, 10 g	19	2	3
Rice Bubbles™, 1 cup, 30 g	83	0	26

FOOD	GI	Fat	CHO
		(grams per serve)	
Breakfast cereals *(continued)*			
Rice Chex, 1 cup, 30 g	89	0	25
Rice Krispies, 1 cup, 30 g	82	0	
Shredded wheat, 1/3 cup, 25 g	67	0	18
Special K™, 1 cup, 30 g	54	0	21
Sultana Bran™, 1 cup, 45 g	52	1	28
Sustain™, 1/2 cup, 30 g	68	2	32
Team™, 30 g	82	0	25
Total™, 30 g	76	0	22
Vita Brits™, 2 biscuits, 30 g	61	1	21
Weett-Bix™, 2 biscuits, 30 g	69	1	19
Wheatbites™, 30 g	72	1	22
Breakfast Bar, Fibre Plus, Uncle Tobys, 1 bar, 42.5 g	78	4	29
Breton wheat crackers, 6 biscuits, 25 g	67	6	14
Broad beans, frozen, boiled, 1/2 cup, 80 g	79	1	9
Buckwheat, cooked, 1/2 cup, 80 g	54(av)	3	57
Bulgur, cooked, 2/3 cup, 120 g	48(av)	0	22
Bun, hamburger, 1 prepacked bun, 50 g	61	3	24
Butter beans, boiled, 1/2 cup, 70g	31(av)	0	13
Cakes			
Angel food cake, 1 slice, 30 g	67	0	17
Banana cake, 1 slice, 80 g	47	7	46
Flan, 1 slice, 80 g	65	5	55
Pound cake, 1 slice, 80 g	54	15	42

FOOD	GI	Fat	CHO
		(grams per serve)	
Cakes *(continued)*			
Sponge cake, 1 slice, 60 g	46	4	32
Calrose white rice, cooked, 1 cup, 180 g	87	1	62
Capellini pasta, boiled, 1 cup, 180 g	45	0	53
Carrots, peeled, boiled, 1/2 cup, 70 g	49	0	3
Cereal grains			
Barley, pearled, boiled, 1/2 cup, 80 g	25 (av)	1	17
Buckwheat, cooked, 1/2 cup, 80 g	54 (av)	3	57
Bulgur, cooked, 2/3 cup, 120 g	48 (av)	1	21
Couscous, cooked, 2/3 cup, 120 g	65 (av)	0	28
Maize			
Cornmeal, wholegrain, cooked, 1/3 cup, 40 g	68	1	30
Sweet corn, canned, drained, 1/2 cup, 80 g	55 (av)	1	15
Taco shells, 2 shells, 26 g	68	6	16
Millet Ragi, cooked, 1/2 cup, 120 g	71	0	12
Rice			
Basmati, white, boiled, 1 cup, 180 g	58	0	50
Calrose, white, cooked, 1 cup 180 g	87	1	62
Doongara white (Mahatma Premium Classic), cooked, 1 cup, 180 g	59	0	59
Instant, cooked, 1 cup, 180 g	87	0	38
Pelde, brown, boiled, 1 cup, 180 g	76	2	57
Sunbrown Quick™, boiled, 1 cup, 180 g	80	3	59

FOOD	GI	Fat	CHO
		(grams per serve)	
Cereal grains *(continued)*			
Tapioca			
(boiled with milk), 1 cup, 265 g	81	6	54
Cheerios ™, breakfast cereal, 30 g	74	2	20
Cherries, 20 cherries, 80 g	22	0	10
Chickpeas, canned, drained, 1/2 cup, 95 g	42	2	15
Chickpeas, boiled, 120 g	33 (av)	3	22
Chocolate, milk, 6 squares, 30 g	49	8	19
Cocopops™ breakfast cereal, 3/4 cup, 30 g	77	0	26
Cordial, orange, diluted, 1 cup, 250 ml	66	0	20
Corn bran, breakfast cereal, 1/2 cup, 30 g	75	1	20
Corn Chex , breakfast cereal, 30 g	83	0	25
Corn chips, toasted, 50 g	72	13	25
Cornflakes, breakfast cereal, 1 cup, 30 g	84 (av)	0	26
Cornmeal (maizemeal), cooked, 1/3 cup, 40 g	68	0	37
Couscous, cooked, 2/3 cup, 120 g	65 (av)	0	28
Crackers			
Breton wheat crackers, 6 biscuits, 25 g	67	6	14
Jatz, 6 biscuits, 25 g	55	5	17
Kavli™, 4 biscuits, 20 g	71	0	13
Premium soda crackers, 3 biscuits, 25 g	74	4	17
Puffed crispbread, 4 biscuits, wholemeal, 20 g	81	1	15
Rice cakes, 2 cakes, 25 g	82	1	21
Ryvita™, 2 slices, 20 g	69	1	16

FOOD	GI	Fat	CHO
		(grams per serve)	
Crackers *(continued)*			
Sao (3 biscs), 25 g	70	4	17
Stoned wheat thins, 5 biscuits, 25 g	67	2	17
Water cracker, Arnotts, 5 biscuits, 25 g	78	2	18
Crispix, breakfast cereal, 30 g	87	1	26
Croissant, 1	67	14	27
Crumpet, 1, toasted, 50 g	69	0	22
Custard, 3/4 cup, 175 g	43	5	24
Dairy foods			
Ice cream, full fat, 2 scoops, 50 g	61 (av)	6	10
Ice cream, low fat, 2 scoops, 50 g	50	2	13
Milk, full fat, 1 cup, 250 ml	27 (av)	10	12
Milk, skim, 1 cup, 250 ml	32	0	13
Milk chocolate, low fat, 1 cup, 250 ml	34	3	23
Custard, 3/4 cup, 175 g	43	5	24
Tofu Frozen Dessert (non-dairy), 100 g	115	1	13
Vitari (non-dairy), frozen fruit product, 80 g	28	0	18
Yoghurt			
low fat, fruit, 200 g	33	0	26
low fat, artificial sweetener, 200 g	14	0	12
Dark rye bread, Blackbread, 1 slice, 50 g	76	1	21
Dark rye bread, Schinkenbröt, 1 slice, 50 g	86	1	22
Digestive biscuits, 2 plain, 30 g	59 (av)	6	21
Donut with cinnamon and sugar, 40 g	76	8	16

FOOD	GI	Fat	CHO
		(grams per serve)	
Doongara white rice (Mahatma Premium Classic), cooked, 1 cup, 180 g	59	0	59
Fanta™, soft drink, 1 can, 375 ml	68	0	51
Fettucini, cooked, 1 cup, 180 g	32	1	57
Fish fingers , oven-cooked, 5 x 25 g fingers, 125 g	38	14	24
Flan cake, 1 slice, 80 g	65	5	55
French baguette bread, 30 g	95	0	15
French fries, fine cut, small serve, 120 g	75	26	49
Fructose, pure, 10 g	23 (av)	0	10
Fruit cocktail, canned in natural juice, 1/2 cup, 125 g	55	0	15
Fruit loaf, heavy, 1 slice, 35 g	47	1	18
Fruits and fruit products			
Apple, 1 medium, 150 g	38 (av)	0	18
Apple juice, unsweetened, 1 cup, 250 ml	40	0	33
Apricots, fresh, 3 medium, 100 g	57	0	7
canned, light syrup, 1/2 cup, 125 g	64	0	13
dried, 5-6 pieces, 30 g	31	0	13
Banana, raw, 1 medium, 150 g	55 (av)	0	32
Cherries, 20 cherries, 80 g	22	0	10
Fruit cocktail, canned in natural juice, 1/2 cup, 125 g	55	0	15
Grapefruit, raw, 1/2 medium, 100 g	25	0	5

FOOD	GI	Fat	CHO
		(grams per serve)	
Fruits and fruit products *(continued)*			
Grapefruit juice, unsweetened, 1 cup, 250 ml	48	0	16
Grapes, green, 1 cup, 100 g)	46 (av)	0	15
Kiwi fruit, 1 raw, peeled, 80 g	52 (av)	0	8
Mango, 1 small, 150 g	55 (av)	0	19
Orange, 1 medium, 130 g	44 (av)	0	10
Orange juice, 1 cup, 250 ml	46	0	21
Paw paw, 1/2 small, 200 g	58 (av)	0	14
Peach, fresh, 1 large, 110 g	42 (av)	0	7
canned, natural juice, 1/2 cup, 125 g	30	0	12
canned, light syrup, 1/2 cup, 125 g	52	0	18
canned, heavy syrup, 1/2 cup, 125 g	58	0	19
Pear, fresh, 1 medium, 150 g	38 (av)	0	21
canned in pear juice, 1/2 cup, 125 g	44	0	13
Pineapple, fresh, 2 slices, 125 g	66	0	10
Pineapple juice, unsweetened, canned, 250 g	46	0	27
Plums, 3-4 small, 100 g	39 (av)	0	7
Raisins, 1/4 cup, 40 g	64	0	28
Rockmelon, raw, 1/4 small, 200 g	65	0	10
Sultanas, 1/4 cup, 40 g	56	0	30
Watermelon, 1 cup, 150 g	72	0	8
Gatorade sports drink, 1 cup, 250 ml	78	0	15
Glucose powder, Glucodin™, 10 g	102	0	10
Gluten-free bread, 1 slice, 30 g	90	1	14

FOOD	GI	Fat	CHO
		(grams per serve)	
Gnocchi, cooked, 1 cup, 145 g	68	3	71
Graham Wafer biscuits, 4 biscuits, 30 g	74	3	22
Grapefruit juice unsweetened, 1 cup, 250 ml	48	0	16
Grapefruit, raw, 1/2 medium, 100 g	25	0	5
Grapes, green, 1 cup, 100 g	46 (av)	0	15
Green gram dhal, 1/2 cup, 100 g	62	4	10
Green gram, soaked and boiled, 120 g	38	1	18
Green pea soup, canned, ready to serve, 220 ml	66	1	22
Hamburger bun, 1 prepacked bun, 50 g	61	3	24
Haricot (navy beans), boiled, 1/2 cup, 90 g	38 (av)	0	11
Honey & Oat Bread (Vogel's™), 1 slice, 40 g	55	3	17
Honey, 1 tablespoon, 20 g	58	0	16
Ice cream, full fat, 2 scoops, 50 g	61 (av)	6	10
Ice cream, low fat, 2 scoops, 50 g	50	2	13
Isostar, sports drink, 1 cup, 250 ml	73	0	18
Jatz crackers, 6 biscuits, 25 g	55	5	17
Jelly beans, 5, 10 g	80	0	9
Kaiser rolls, 1 roll, 50 g	73	1	25
Kavli™ crackers, 4 biscuits, 20 g	71	0	13
Kidney beans, boiled, 1/2 cup, 90 g	27 (av)	0	18
Kidney beans, canned and drained, 1/2 cup, 95 g	52	0	13
Kiwi fruit, 1 raw, peeled, 70-80 g	52 (av)	0	8
Lactose, pure, 10 g	46 (av)	0	10
Lentil soup, canned, 220 ml	44	0	14

FOOD	GI	Fat	CHO
		(grams per serve)	
Lentils, green and brown, dried, boiled, 1/2 cup, 95 g	30 (av)	0	16
Lentils, red, boiled, 120 g	26 (av)	1	21
Life Savers™, 5 peppermint, 10 g	70	0	10
Light rye bread, 1 slice, 50 g	68	1	23
Lima beans, baby, frozen, 1/2 cup, 85 g	32	0	17
Linguine pasta, thick, cooked, 1 cup, 180 g	46 (av)	1	56
Linguine pasta, thin, cooked, 1 cup, 180 g	55 (av)	1	56
Linseed rye bread, 1 slice, 50 g	55	5	21
Liquid meals			
Sustagen Sport (diluted as directed), 1 cup, 250 ml	43	0	50
Lucozade™, original, 1 bottle, 300 ml	95	<1	56
Lungkow bean thread, 180 g	26	0	61
Macaroni and cheese, packaged, cooked, 220 g	64	24	30
Macaroni, cooked, 1 cup, 180 g	45	1	56
Maize			
Cornmeal, wholegrain, 1/3 cup, 40 g	68	1	30
Sweet corn, canned and drained, 1/2 cup, 80 g	55 (av)	1	15
Maltose (maltodextrins), pure, 10 g	105	0	10
Mango, 1 small, 150 g	55 (av)	0	19
Mars Bar™, 60 g	68	11	41
Melba toast, 4 squares, 30 g	70	1	19
Milk, full fat, 1 cup, 250 ml	27 (av)	10	12

FOOD	GI	Fat	CHO
		(grams per serve)	
Milk, skim, 1 cup, 250 ml	32	0	13
chocolate flavoured, 1 cup, 250 ml	34	9	23
Milk Arrowroot biscuits, 2 biscuits, 16 g	63	2	13
Millet, cooked, 1/2 cup, 120 g	71	0	12
Mini Wheats™ (whole wheat) breakfast			
cereal, 1 cup, 30 g	58	0	21
Morning Coffee biscuits, 3 biscuits, 18 g	79	2	14
Muesli Bars with fruit, 30 g	61	4	17
Muesli, breakfast cereal			
toasted, 1/2 cup, 60 g	43	9	33
non-toasted, 1/2 cup, 60 g	56	6	32
Muffins			
Apple, 1 muffin, 80 g	44	10	44
Bran, 1 muffin, 80 g	60	8	34
Blueberry, 1 muffin, 80 g	59	8	41
Noodles, 2-minute, 1 x 85 g packet, cooked	46	16	55
Nutella (spread), 20 g	33	6	12
Nutri-grain™ breakfast cereal, 1 cup, 30 g	66	0	20
Oat Bran & Honey Loaf Bread (Burgen™)			
with Barley, 1 slice, 40 g	31	2	14
Oat bran, 1 tablespoon, 10 g	55	1	7
Oat bran breakfast cereal, 2/3 cup, 30 g		3	20
Oatmeal biscuits, 3 biscuits, 30 g	54	6	19
Orange , 1 medium, 130 g	44 (av)	0	10

FOOD	GI	Fat	CHO
		(grams per serve)	
Orange cordial, diluted, 1 cup, 250 ml	66	0	20
Orange juice, 1 cup, 250 ml	46	0	21
Parsnips, boiled, 1/2 cup, 75 g	97	0	8
Pasta			
Capellini, cooked, 1 cup, 180 g	45	0	53
Fettucini, cooked, 1 cup, 180 g	32	1	57
Gnocchi, cooked, 1 cup, 145 g	68		
Noodles, 2-minute, 85 g packet, cooked	46	16	55
Linguine thick, cooked, 1 cup, 180 g	46 (av)	1	56
Linguine thin, cooked, 1 cup, 180 g	55 (av)	1	56
Macaroni , cooked, 1 cup, 180 g	45	1	56
Macaroni and cheese, packaged,			
cooked, 220 g	64	24	30
Ravioli, meat-filled, cooked, 1 cup, 220 g	39	11	30
Rice pasta, brown, cooked, 1 cup, 180 g	92	2	57
Spaghetti, white, cooked, 1 cup, 180 g	41 (av)	1	56
Spaghetti, wholemeal, cooked, 1 cup, 180 g	37 (av)	1	48
Spirali, durum, cooked, 1 cup, 180 g	43	1	56
Star Pastina, cooked, 1 cup, 180 g	38		
Tortellini, cheese, cooked, 180 g	50	8	21
Vermicelli, cooked, 1 cup, 180 g	35	0	45
Pastry, flaky, 65 g	59	26	25
Paw paw, raw, 1/2 small, 200 g	58 (av)	0	14
Pea and ham soup, canned, 220 ml	66	2	40

FOOD	GI	Fat	CHO
		(grams per serve)	
Peach, fresh, 1 large, 110 g	42 (av)	0	7
canned, natural juice, 1/2 cup, 125 g	30	0	12
canned, heavy syrup, 1/2 cup, 125 g	58	0	19
canned, light syrup, 1/2 cup, 125 g	52	0	18
Peanuts, roasted, salted, 1/2 cup, 75 g	14 (av)	40	11
Pear fresh, 1 medium, 150 g	38 (av)	0	21
canned in pear juice, 1/2 cup, 125 g	44	0	13
Peas, green, fresh, frozen, boiled, 1/2 cup, 80 g	48 (av)	0	5
Peas dried, boiled, 1/2 cup, 70 g	22	0	4
Pelde brown rice, boiled, 1 cup, 180 g	76	2	57
Pineapple , fresh, 2 slices, 125 g	66	0	10
Pineapple juice, unsweetened, canned, 250 g	46	0	27
Pinto beans, canned, 1/2 cup, 95 g	45	0	13
Pinto beans, soaked, boiled, 1/2 cup, 90 g	39	0	20
Pita bread, 1 piece, 65 g	57	1	38
Pizza, cheese and tomato, 2 slices, 230 g	60	27	57
Ploughman's Bread, without grainy bits, wholemeal, 2 slices, 90 g	47	1	21
Ploughman's Loaf™, mixed grain bread, 1 slice, 45 g	47	1	21
Plums, 3–4 small, 100 g	39 (av)	0	7
Popcorn, low fat, 2 cups (popped), 20 g	55	2	10
Porridge (made with water), 1 cup, 245 g	42	2	24

FOOD	GI	Fat	CHO
		(grams per serve)	
Potatoes			
French Fries, fine cut, small serve, 120 g	75	26	49
instant potato	83 (av)	1	18
new, peeled, boiled, 5 small (cocktail), 175 g	62 (av)	0	23
new, canned, drained, 5 small 175 g	61	0	20
pale skin, peeled, boiled, 1 medium, 120 g	56 (av)	0	16
pale skin, baked in oven (no fat), 1 medium, 120 g	85 (av)	0	14
pale skin, mashed, 1/2 cup, 120 g	70 (av)	0	16
pale skin, steamed, 1 medium, 120 g	65	0	17
pale skin, microwaved, 1 medium, 120 g	82	0	17
Pontiac, boiled,	56	0	16
potato crisps, plain, 50 g	54 (av)	16	24
Potato crisps, plain, 50 g	54 (av)	16	24
Pound cake, 1 slice, 80 g	54	15	42
Pretzels, 50 g	83	1	22
Puffed crispbread, 4 wholemeal, 20 g	81	1	15
Puffed Wheat breakfast cereal, Sanitarium, 1 cup, 30 g	80	1	22
Pumpernickel bread, 2 slices	41	2	35
Pumpkin, peeled, boiled, 1/2 cup, 85 g	75	0	6
Raisins, 1/4 cup, 40 g	64	0	28
Ravioli, meat-filled, cooked, 1/2 cup, 220 g	39	11	30

FOOD	GI	Fat	CHO
			(grams per serve)
Rice			
Basmati ,white, boiled, I cup, 180 g	58	0	50
Calrose, white, cooked, I cup 180 g	87	I	62
Doongara white (Mahatma Premium Classic), cooked, I cup, 180 g	59	0	59
Instant, cooked, I cup, 180 g	87	0	38
Pelde, brown, boiled, I cup, 180g	76	2	57
Sunbrown Quick™, boiled, I cup, 180g	80	3	59
Rice bran, I tablespoon, 10 g	19	2	3
Rice Bubbles™, I cup, 30 g	83	0	26
Rice cakes, 2 cakes, 25 g	82	I	21
Rice Chex, breakfast cereal, 30 g	89	0	25
Rice Krispies, breakfast cereal, 30 g	82	0	27
Rice pasta, brown, cooked, I cup, 180 g	92	2	57
Rice vermicelli, cooked, 180 g	58	0	58
Rich Tea biscuits, 2 biscuits, 20 g	55	3	16
Rockmelon, raw, 1/4 small, 200 g	65	0	6
Roggenbrot™ bread (Vogel's™), I slice, 35-40 g	59	I	17
Roll (bread), Kaiser, I roll, 50 g	73	I	25
Romano beans, boiled, 1/2 cup, 90 g	46	0	21
Rye bread, I slice, 50 g	65	I	23
Ryvita™ crackers, 2 biscuits, 20 g	69	I	16
Sao crackers, 3 biscuits, 25 g	70	4	17
Sausages, fried, 2, 120 g	28	21	6

FOOD	GI	Fat	CHO
			(grams per serve)
Semolina, cooked, 1 cup, 230 g	55	0	17
Shortbread , 2 biscuits, 30 g	64	8	19
Shredded wheat breakfast cereal, 1/3 cup, 25 g	67	0	18
Shredded Wheatmeal biscuits, 2 biscuits, 16 g	62	2	12
So Good™, 1 cup, 250 ml	31	9	12
Soda crackers, 3 biscuits, 25 g	74	4	17
Soft drink, Fanta™, 1 can, 375 ml	68	0	51
Soups			
Black bean soup, 220 ml	64	2	82
Green pea soup, canned, ready to serve, 220 ml	66	1	22
Lentil soup, canned, 220 ml	44	0	14
Pea and ham soup, 220 ml	60	2	13
Tomato soup, canned, 220 ml	38	1	15
Sourdough rye bread, 1 slice, 50 g	57	2	23
Soya beans, canned, 1/2 cup, 100 g	14	6	12
Soya beans, boiled, 1/2 cup, 90 g	18 (av)	7	10
Spaghetti , white, cooked, 1 cup, 180 g	41 (av)	1	56
Spaghetti, wholemeal, cooked, 1 cup, 180 g	37 (av)	1	48
Special K™, 1 cup, 30 g	54	0	21
Spirali, durum, cooked, 1 cup, 180 g	43	1	56
Split pea soup, 220 ml	60	0	6
Split peas, yellow, boiled, 1/2 cup, 90 g	32	0	16
Sponge cake plain, 1 slice, 60 g	46	16	32

FOOD	GI	Fat	CHO
		(grams per serve)	
Sports drinks			
Gatorade, 1 cup, 250 ml	78	0	15
Isostar, 1 cup, 250ml	70	0	18
Sportsplus, 1 cup, 250 ml	74	0	17
Sustagen Sport drink (diluted as directed),			
60 g in 165 ml water	43	0	40
Stoned wheat thins crackers, 5 biscuits, 25 g	67	2	17
Sucrose, 1 teaspoon	65 (av)	0	5
Sultana Bran™, 1 cup, 45 g	52	1	35
Sultanas, 1/4 cup, 40 g	56	0	30
Sunbrown Quick™ rice, boiled, 1 cup, 180 g	80	3	59
Sunflower & Barley bread (Riga), 1 slice, 40 g	57	1	17
Sustain™, 1/2 cup, 30 g	68	1	25
Swede, peeled, boiled, 60 g	72	0	3
Sweet corn, 1/2 cup, 85 g	55 (av)	1	16
Sweet potato, peeled, boiled, 80 g	54 (av)	0	16
Taco shells, 2 shells, 26 g	68	6	16
Tapioca pudding, boiled with milk, 1 cup, 250 g	81	10.5	51
Tapioca, steamed 1 hour, 100 g	70	6	54
Taro, peeled, boiled, 80 g	54	0	19
Team™ breakfast cereal, 30 g	82	0	25
Tofu Frozen Dessert (non-dairy), 100 g	115	1	13
Tomato soup, canned, 220 ml	38	1	15
Tortellini, cheese, cooked, 180 g	50	8	21

FOOD	GI	Fat	CHO
		(grams per serve)	
Total™ breakfast cereal, 30 g	76	0	22
Vanilla wafer biscuits, 6 biscuits, 30 g	77	5	21
Vermicelli, cooked, 1 cup, 180 g	35	0	45
Vita Brits™, breakfast cereal, 2 biscuits, 30 g	61	1	21
Vitari, non-dairy frozen fruit product, 80 g	28	0	18
Waffles, 25 g	76	3	9
Water crackers, 5 biscuits, 25 g	78	2	18
Watermelon, 1 cup, 150 g	72	0	8
Weet-Bix™ breakfast cereal, 2 biscuits, 30 g	69	1	19
Wheatbites™, breakfast cereal, 30 g	72	1	22
White bread, wheat flour, 1 slice, 30 g	70 (av)	1	15
Wholemeal bread, wheat flour, 1 slice, 35 g	69 (av)	1	14
Wonderwhite™(with Hi-Maize™)			
bread, 1 slice, 35 g	80	1	17
Yam, boiled, 80 g	51	0	26
Yoghurt			
low fat, fruit, 200 g	33	0	26
low fat, artificial sweetener, 200 g	14	0	12

HOW TO FIND A SPORTS DIETITIAN

- The best way to obtain the names of sports dietitians practising in your area is to contact:

  Sports Dietitians Australia
  Level 8, Victorian Institute of Sport
  20–22 Albert Road, South Melbourne
  P.O. Box 828, South Melbourne, 3205
  Telephone (03) 9682 2442
  Fax (03) 9686 2352

- It is also worth checking in the *Yellow Pages* for your area.
- Most state institutes of sport have sports dietitians consulting with their athletes.

RECOMMENDED READING ON SPORTS NUTRITION

For an expanded discussion on sports nutrition the following books are highly recommended.

Burke L., *The Complete Guide to Food for Sports Performance*, Allan and Unwin 1995

Cardwell G., *Gold Medal Nutrition.*, Glenn Cardwell 1996 (self published)

Garden L., *Footy Food*, Lorna Garden 1993.

O'Connor H and Hay D., *The Taste of Fitness*, JB Fairfax Press 1993

Roberts C and Inge K., *Food for Sport Cookbook*, Rene Gordon 1993

ABOUT THE AUTHORS

Helen O'Connor, a sports dietitian and lecturer in the Department of Exercise and Sport Science at the University of Sydney. Helen consults at the Sydney Sports Medicine Centre, Olympic Park and at the Sydney Academy of Sport. She is the personal dietitian for the Sydney Swans, Super League Canterbury and a number of Australia's elite athletes.

Associate Professor Jennie Brand Miller, a member of the teaching and research staff of the Human Nutrition Unit at the University of Sydney, is a world authority on the glycaemic index of foods. Her most recent book was *The G.I. Factor* (Hodder & Stoughton, 1996).

Dr Stephen Colagiuri, Director of the Diabetes Centre and Head of the Department of Endocrinology, Metabolism and Diabetes at the Prince of Wales Hospital, Sydney, has published extensively on carbohydrate in the diet of people with diabetes. His most recent book was *The G.I. Factor*.

Kaye Foster-Powell, an accredited practising dietitian-nutritionist, is the senior dietitian at Wentworth Area Diabetes Service and conducts a private practice. Her most recent book was *The G.I. Factor*.

PARENTING
TEENS

Nancy Van Pelt

First published 2009

© 2009

All rights reserved. No part of this publication may be reproduced in any form without prior permission from the publisher.

British Library Cataloguing in Publication Data.
A catalogue record for this book is available from the British Library.

ISBN 978-1-906381-46-2

Published by Autumn House,
Grantham, Lincolnshire.

Printed in Thailand.

Teens

The origin of the word teen is the old English word *teona*.

It means injury, anger and grief.

The teen years can be painful for both teen and parent.

Suspended in time

Although a teen has not yet earned the freedom of adulthood, he has lost the privileges of childhood.

As a result, for seven years, he finds himself suspended in time.

The average 15-year-old feels as though everything he finds appealing is prohibited.

Worse than before?

The media overflow with statistics on juvenile crime, delinquency, teen pregnancy and drug abuse.

Are teens today worse than we were?

Not *worse*, but it is safe to say that teens today definitely differ from the teens of twenty or thirty years ago.

The difference

Teens today do very much
the same things as we did,
but they do them at an earlier
age than ever before.

Sociologists confirm that
children grow up faster. They
date earlier and are introduced
to all facets of life at an early
age.

More money

Teens have more money, more access to transport, more leisure time, and less supervision than ever before.

They also mature sexually three years earlier than the past generation.

Adult problems

The difficulties with teens are compounded by adult problems. Divorce, inflation, energy crises and political corruption are not pretty pictures.

Adults who cannot handle their own difficulties are hardly equipped to cope with the problems erupting inside a teen.

Through this difficult time, a teen needs parents who can recognise that he is changing into an adult rather than parents who overreact to teen attitudes and behaviours.

Easily upset

Until the teen years, your youngster has more or less accepted your guidance, at least after a little persuasion.

Now, however, you may notice that he wants every sentence verified.

The child who once seemed so content in your care now seems troubled, restless and easily upset.

Appropriate discipline

The methods of discipline you previously used now seem heavy-handed. Your teenager's self-esteem takes a nosedive.

The closeness you dreamed of maintaining with your teen seems unattainable.

The active listening you've been saving to use isn't working as you thought it would. . . .

Mentally absent

Your teen does not want to stay at home with the family any more.

When he is at home, he seems to be mentally absent. His mind has wandered off. At time he acts as though it is a crime to be seen in your presence. . . .

Highs and lows

The teen's emotional highs and lows, bursts of temper and periods of sluggishness confuse you.

You wonder whether you are losing your touch as parents.

Your challenge is to understand yourself *and* your teen.

Storms come and go

Storms come.

You try hard to remember what it was like when you were young. You listen to scary stories your friends relate about how they failed to cope when difficult times came.

Fortified with little hope of success, you bravely turn your face into the storm. . . .

Only to discover that the current deluge is over but a new one is brewing.

It's normal!

If this even partially describes your home, relax. It's normal! You need not feel as though you are failing as a parent because you find yourself embroiled by emotional struggles with your emerging adolescents. You are experiencing the early process of rebellion.

What's rebellion?

By definition, rebellion refers to resistance or rejection of authority or control.

Pause a moment. . . .

Ask yourself what would happen if your child never resisted or rejected your control.

Preparing for independence

During the teen years the emerging adult begins to extricate himself from his parents' values, ideas and controls – and attempts to establish his own.

This is a necessary process. It is a process of establishing one's own individuality, code of ethics, values, ideas and beliefs.

Timing varies

For some teens the process occurs earlier than others. For some it will be a difficult transition; for others it will be comparatively easy. Parents of the latter group stand around scratching their heads as they listen to the wild stories of parents who feel they've been to hell and back with their teenagers.

It's necessary!

For all teenagers the process of
establishing one's own identity is
a necessary procedure.

If it does not transpire during the teen
years when it is supposed to, it will
probably occur at some future time.
For instance, during mid-life. Many
mid-life crisis situations might actually
be termed latent periods of rebellion.

Recognition

Through rebellion the teenager
cries out for recognition of
his individuality. He no longer
wants you to consider him
your property, but nonetheless
he remains your responsibility.

He is attempting to find
out who he is and what he
stands for.

On the line

Both his identity and self-respect are on the line. In his search to find these answers he may react more strongly to your authority than he previously did. You would be wise to recognise that his reaction is *not* something personal against you, but something *normal* developing within him.

Yes, rebellion is normal!

Normal rebellion will lead the adolescent to a mature life. This constructive time period will assist the teenager in shedding childish ways and developing independence.

The challenge is to keep the lines of communication open at all times.

Coping skills

Remember, your teen remains a novice in coping with his own feelings as well as in coping with your feelings and reactions.

Both parent and teen *must* remain open to exploring persistent problems.

Communicate!

Mood swings

Your teen's mood swings may frustrate you. Sometimes he behaves as if he is 'king of the mountain'. Before you adjust to that mood, he's plummeted into the abyss of despair and hopeless despondency.

To teens all facets of life appear greatly magnified or exaggerated.

'I've told you a million times . . .'

Because the teen experiences exaggerated attitudes and moods, it is important that you do not.

Everything is either great or awful, the coldest or the hottest, the most wonderful or the most detestable.

Your actions count
In the face of your teen's irrationality, the maturity of your actions and reactions will help him recognise that life is 10% what happens to a person and 90% how he reacts to it.

Multidirectional

Teens don't pause long enough to look for long in any given direction. One day he may walk a mile to see Julie. In a few weeks he may walk two miles to avoid seeing her. One day he can't get his fill of pizza. The next day he can't understand what all the fuss is about.

Budget for irrationality!

Watch your reactions

Your teen may talk back to you, argue with you, test rules and curfews, question religion, and reject long-established family values. He may demonstrate the same challenge to authority through his clothes and his music.

The trick is not to overreact.

Don't dictate!

Whether your teen's rebellious period remains within the confines of 'normal' or whether it becomes abnormal in its intensity and direction, depends to a large extent on the way you react to it. If you redouble your efforts to dictate and control, the seeds of insurrection may take root deep inside your child.

If you continue to dictate . . .

You are simply storing up trouble for the future.

You may be able to control him for a limited time, but he will probably vow that some day, somehow, he will get even with you.

Show him patience, and he will find himself.

So what's 'abnormal rebellion'?

Abnormal rebellion bogs down the family in constant battles over the car, dates, friends, curfews, rules or money. A cold war rages in the home where family members fear to speak lest they escalate rebellion. Abnormal rebellion takes a teenager out of the mainstream of life.

Lines of communication

Keeping the lines of communication open avoids the escalation of rebellion. If rebellion escalates it leads to a narrow detour that can lead to a life seething with bitterness and hate.

Degree and frequency

Abnormal rebellion can be measured in terms of degree and frequency. In one district some teens drove sports cars across lawns, uprooted shrubs, broke windows, smeared walls with paint, smashed plaster with hatchets.

Does that put your teen problems into perspective?

Beating the system

In an effort to 'beat the system' some teens resort to theft. They steal not from the need but for the thrill of it.

Their real need is attention.

They're saying to their parents, 'Now maybe I can get you to pay some attention to me.'

Abnormal rebellion

Involves a total refusal to co-operate in family or social responsibilities.

Rebellion becomes abnormal when a teenager refuses to abide by reasonable household rules: ignores curfews, habitually experiments with alcohol, drugs and/or sex, or has repeated brushes with the law.

Siblings

The younger the teenager who resorts to the abnormal rebellious stage, the more difficult it is for the remainder of the family – particularly younger children. They may seek to emulate the behaviour they witness.

In these circumstances the worst thing you can do is overreact.

By the book?

It is a mistake to believe that when you've raised your children 'by the book' there will be no problems.

Begin by separating what you are responsible for and what your teen is responsible for. You can only do so much. And you can always pray.

Does abnormal rebellion reflect on the parent?

Not necessarily. It can happen in the best-regulated homes of the most devout Christians.

You need not feel responsible for *everything* an irresponsible teen does.

If he chooses to make irresponsible choices regardless of your warnings, then he must reap the consequences of his own decisions. You can only do your best.

'The family that prays together . . .'?

The Bible, family worship, Christian schools, regular church attendance, parental example, and consistency are essential and helpful in rearing children, *but these do not guarantee that our children will turn out well.*

In parenting there are no guarantees.

No control freakery

No parent can or should control his teen's destiny.

Just as God leaves us free to make certain choices, so we should allow our teens freedom to make some decisions.

Be ready to forgive
God always welcomes
us back when we
repent and ask for
forgiveness.

Be quick to forgive
your prodigals!

Unconditional love

What do you do when teens test their religious values by attempting to reject yours?

You make sure they understand that they are still part – and a valued part at that – of the loved family circle.

Family evenings

In the week there may be heated words or a bad scene or two. But on Friday evenings we should always embrace all members of the family. All need to know that they are loved and that they belong.

No matter how rebellious he is –

Make sure that your teen receives the message of unconditional love. Even if he does not return it, it means more than you can ever know.

God never withdraws his love from us. And since parents, in a sense, stand in the place of God to their children, they must be able to demonstrate this kind of unconditional, indestructible love to a rebellious teenager, no matter how difficult it may be.

Broad principles

There are several broad principles that may help you as you guide your teen through this demanding period.

The first principle: Learn to communicate.

Set aside the endless verbal battles that tend to leave you exhausted and discouraged.

No shouting

Shouting only weakens your authority and provides a strategic advantage for your teen. Look for better ways.

Serious conference

A crisis situation demands
a serious conference with
your teenager. Don't conduct
it in a public place. Convey,
without blaming or judging,
the seriousness of the
situation. Explain the need
to establish one's own
identity and values.

The limits of freedom

Your teen desires more and more freedom. Explain that you cannot set him free to do whatever he wishes. As a parent you have a God-given responsibility to guide and protect him – even though he's a teenager.

Apologise when you're at fault

Sincere parental apology can go a long way with a teen. It actually builds his respect for you and restores the bond between you. Apologise when you lose your cool, overreact, or act unwisely.

Clarity
Aim for clarity in all
your communication
with teens.

State your intentions
to correct unacceptable
behaviour and explain
exactly what is wrong
with it.

Frontiers of behaviour

Define the frontiers of behaviour. Set limits. Let your teenager know that even though he is growing up and will soon be on his own, this does not mean that he can be on his own in your home.

Rules and sanctions

All must abide by certain general rules for family living in order for peace and harmony to abound. Make the rules clear and simple.

Innumerate the rules on which you will not compromise. Then calmly let your teen know that if he chooses deliberately to disobey you from this point on, you will have to resort to drastic measures. You may have to explain what these are.

Love

Convey your entire message in love. Reassure your teen of your concern and deep love. Tell him that you want a happy home during your few remaining years left together as a family.

Ask for co-operation

Ask for your teen's
co-operation in
achieving a peaceful
family atmosphere
and in shouldering his
responsibilities around
the home. If you
respect him, his respect
for himself and for you
may be fostered.

Tough love

If you do all this and your teen remains hostile and defiant, you may have to resort to tough love. Indeed, there is an organisation called ToughLove. It is an international framework for support groups of parents who draw a tough line for problem teens.

The final sanction

The final sanction is to say, 'You have to live in our family as a decent human being or you have to leave.' Parents then give their teens the choice of living with friends, relatives, or other ToughLove parents. To learn more about ToughLove visit *www.toughlove.com.*

Ultimately, trying to control a teen's environment will not work

Even if it is possible for parents to make decisions about the choice of entertainment, friends, clothes, music, reading, TV programmes and movies, and even if they place the teen in a Christian school, they cannot place him beyond the reach of evil influences.

Christian schools have their limits

You cannot completely shield your teen from 'worldly influences'. The same problems that exist in the state school system can be found in Christian schools to a lesser degree. Attempting to isolate a teen from worldly influences is an ineffective method of control. Since such a teen must eventually leave the structured environment, he or she may be the least prepared of all young people to deal with the realities of life.

Overreaction to negative influences

This is a common mistake. Parents hope that by overreacting with negative remarks about non-Christian standards and activities, their teen will avoid such folly in the future.

That technique backfires by producing the opposite effect.

Tuning out

Faced by a pattern of overreaction on the part of their parents, teens will simply tune them out completely. Even when it appears that they are listening respectfully, the likelihood is that outside the home they will pursue what their parents have 'preached' against.

Concealing behaviour

Unknown to parents, teens may also carry out clandestine activities inside the home, having become clever at concealing their behaviour from their parents.

A vicious circle develops. When the parent discovers the concealed behaviour, the reaction – driven by guilt – becomes even more inappropriate.

'The inoculation approach'

This may be the most effective method of teaching values and standards to a teen. Just as parents provide the opportunity for their child to receive small dosages of infectious agents in order to gain immunity from disease, so the parent prepares his child during the early years.

How it works

Rather than preaching against negative influences or isolating the child from them, the parent teaches values through example and open, direct discussion in the face of exposure to what is questionable.

When an issue arises, both the pros and cons are discussed in an open way. The young person is talked *with* (not *to*) and gently guided.

Practising choice

The parent, as often as possible, allows the young person to make his own choices early in the selection process – *even if the decision is poor.* How much better that the young person learns early how to avoid poor choices than later on when decisions have greater consequences.

Atmosphere of openness

Parents find it hard to tolerate an atmosphere of openness, yet it is by far the most effective approach.

However, wise decision-making is an acquired ability. Like a muscle, it must be used repeatedly in order to develop.

Parents must provide the opportunity for its development.

Setting standards

Good parents who wish to try the inoculation method will involve the teen in setting standards for the home in advance of the event. Crucial areas include driving, dating and sexual behaviour.

All must be addressed in discussion.

Advance preparation

Prior to the time a teenager is allowed the privilege of dating or driving, he or she should be encouraged to suggest guidelines to follow when using the car or dating later on. Parents, too, can have input into the agreement, which can then be drawn up.

Written rules

A young person should help to formulate and agree to abide by written rules. He will tend to follow through much more consistently with these kinds of rules formulated in this way.

Time and patience

An approach like this takes time, effort and patience, but rich dividends are the handsome payoff. A teen who has been allowed to make choices is likely to co-operate with family policies and to develop a healthy independence and self-respect.

'Everybody's doing it'
Parents must explain
that everyone does
not do things alike;
therefore they do not
need to know what
other parents or teens
are doing.

Some freedom

Parents should make every effort to be as lenient as possible and, within reason, give their teen the freedom he desires. However, it is very important that Christian parents establish early in their child's life that they do things differently as a whole than non-Christian parents because their value system is different.

Top tip
Once the rules have
been agreed to, the
parent must be careful
to find the teen doing
something right, and
to affirm it.

Don't say 'No' immediately

Parents always feel that they are on safe ground by thinking it over. Always listen to the arguments *before* saying 'No'.

Maybe
When 'No' becomes
'Yes' your no's for
the future will be
interpreted as if you
have said, 'Maybe; . . .
I'll think it over.'

'Give me the facts'

A wise plan is to suggest, 'Give me the facts, and then I'll make a decision.' When the facts have been presented, say, 'I really haven't made a decision yet. Give me some time to think it over. I want to talk with your dad (or mum), and I'll let you know when we decide.'

That way you make as rational a decision as possible.

Punishment for teenagers

Physical punishments for teens are always inappropriate. Your teen's self-esteem must not be sacrificed on the altar of resentment.

Don't abandon control

On the contrary, give consistent supervision. Your teen's sense of security depends on it.

Talking things through

Talking things through within a matrix of reasoning and concern can adequately handle many infractions. If this process fails, you may decide to withhold privileges – an evening with friends, a trip, the use of the car, and so forth.

Withholding allowances

May help to control some types of misbehaviour, but do not use it to improve failing school grades. Poor grades point to problems that may lie beyond the teen's control.

Give teens a part in setting the rules

Parents might regard this as a calculated attempt to influence behaviour, but to teens it is a fresh breeze on the scene. Faced with a son who consistently came home late at night, a mother said, 'Let's hear you give yourself the lecture you deserve right now.' (The lecture he gave himself was more strongly worded than the one his mother might have given him.)

Working responsibilities

Before a teen can assume the responsibilities of adult life, he needs to learn about life and how to live it. Therefore, wise parents will make their homes a test laboratory where each teen can practise the art of living and homemaking.

Essentials

Every teen should learn to cook, care for the laundry, clean the house, make household repairs, buy groceries, balance a budget, care for the garden, and plan social events.

Responsibility

Teens – boys and girls – can
and should assist with the
preparation of food, and
from time to time take
entire responsibility for the
preparation of the family
meal.

Give them a say
Give teens a say in
home chores. If John
has football practice on
Tuesday night, schedule
his washing-up duties
for a different night.

Co-operation

If Mother and Dad pitch in and help John with the dishes, he would more quickly learn to help others when they are in need.

Outside interests
Parents should be
considerate of a teen's
outside interests – if,
of course, the teen
remembers his home
obligations.

Part-time jobs
If the teen has a part-time job it will offer him a sense of prestige as well as a source of income and may help him to choose a career.

In trouble

A study among teens indicated that almost 88% of those who had been in trouble with the law had answered, 'Nothing' when asked this question: 'What do you do in your spare time?'

How to motivate a teen

The teen years are a self-centred time of life when rewards appeal to young people. If you feel that your teen needs motivating, the following may be helpful:

1
Choose a motivator which is important to your teen

Motivators can include limited use of the car, a special article of clothing, and arrangements such as, 'Yes, you can have what you want, but you will have to earn it.'

2
Formalise the agreement

Draw up a written contract which both teen and parents sign. Driving a car calls for accountability, and if your teen is to drive he must demonstrate responsibility in other areas of life. Some parents even introduce a points system.

3
Establish a method of providing immediate rewards

Most of us need something tangible to sustain our interest as we move towards a goal. Give teens points according to a fixed scale for each chore. Establish in advance the number of points he will require to earn in order to achieve his objective (driving lessons, an article of clothing, and so on).

Rules for parents . . .

Respect your teen's privacy.
Allow your teen his own space, and do not interfere with personal letters, diaries and phone calls. If you suspect your teen is doing drugs, search and seizure is in order, but not the confiscation of diaries and mail.

Rules for parents . . .

Make the home attractive.
Neat personal appearance, making beds, and a clean kitchen can save a teen embarrassment when friends visit. Remember: a teen is keenly sensitive to his peers' reaction towards his parents.

Never stop doing things together as a family

Some teens have splendid parents, but the only time they see them is when they are being corrected or criticised. Family games, camping trips, holidays, hikes through the woods, building projects and friendly debates create an atmosphere in which young people naturally want to share.

Rules for parents . . .

Supervise subtly.

A teen does not respond to a parade of don'ts, yet inwardly he craves guidance. He is caught between opposing forces. On the one hand he resents spineless parents, but on the other he rebels at the infraction on his freedom, especially when parents become arbitrary over things which he feels he can handle himself.

The anchor of discipline

A teen needs the anchor of parental discipline to hold him. And, as always, discipline should be fair and never divided. No teen should be allowed to play one parent against the other.

Rules for parents . . .

Respect his cry for independence.

A teen needs bonds but not bondage, and parents must distinguish between the two. Everything parents do from infancy on works towards making a teen more dependent or independent – until they work themselves out of a job, not out of a relationship.

Experimentation
When your teen
indicates that he
wants more freedom,
step back a little
and experiment with
limited freedom –
for a limited period.

Rules for parents . . .
**Maintain a sense
of humour.**
Managing a teenager
successfully means
balancing love and
discipline on a scale
of good humour.

A light touch

A teen, or an adult for that matter, will do almost anything within reason when a request or a suggestion is made with a light touch. A sense of humour is an antidote for taking the teen years too seriously.

Laughter

Laughter in the home creates an atmosphere of acceptance and joy, and a teenager needs to learn to enjoy family living and laugh with others and at himself.

Rules for parents . . .

Discuss changes that may take place.

Casually discuss with your teen the changes that take place in adolescence. It is years too late to begin sex education, but sex education should continue through the teen years.

Rules for parents . . .

**Enlist sibling
understanding.**
If you discuss privately
with younger members
of the family areas of
conflict, understanding can
be achieved and trouble
lessened.

Lessons for parents . . .

Listen to your teen.

Presenting your teen with a closed mind and the attitude 'He doesn't know what he's talking about' is destructive of people and families.

Active listening

Listen without getting angry,
without blaming and judging
and without name calling.
Active listening becomes
increasingly important during
teen years in attempting to
close the generation gap.

Rules for parents . . .
Provide security, love and acceptance.

Teens need security in a relationship that doesn't change with circumstances. Teens need to know that even through misunderstandings and differences, their relationships with their parents are never broken –
no matter what.

Letting go
Mature love for a
teenager means that
Mother and Father are
ready to share in the
life and growth of their
child and to release
that growing person
into an ever-enlarging
sphere of existence.

Rules for parents . . .

Provide a model of a happy marriage.

Teens need to see parents expressing their love for one another – daily. During the tumultuous years of adolescence, a teen needs the attention of both a mother and a father.

Parental rights versus teen privileges

Parents have the right to dissuade their teen from associating with questionable friends.

Nevertheless, irrational disapproval will make forbidden friends even more desirable.

Parents have the right to refuse their teen the use of the family car when the parental needs supersede his, or for any other logical reason.

Your teen will have unlimited rights to a car only when he has bought his own.

Parents have the right to control all incoming and outgoing phone calls from all telephones installed and maintained at their expense.

Consistently enforced ground rules are needed.

Parents have the right to deprive their teen of privileges he has not earned.

Teens must keep their side of the bargain!

Parents have the right to expect their teen to do his best in school.

On the other hand, parents have no right to inflict unrealistic expectations on their teens.

Parents have the right to set standards concerning their teen's appearance.

Parents must realise, however, that any campaign designed to thwart the teen who is bent on looking like everyone else is most assuredly doomed. Parents must understand that an adolescent changes the way he looks and dresses in order to differ from his parents, to be conspicuous, and then to fade into the crowd of his peers.

Opposing crazes

The more you oppose each
craze, the more your teen will
pursue each one as it comes
along. As much as is humanly
possible, allow your teen to
select his clothes. He needs
to wear what is important to
him so he can feel accepted
by his group.

If there is a moral issue . . .

Take a firm stand. For example, a suggestive dress or a lack of underclothing. Teen girls do not yet have the knowledge and wisdom to understand how their clothing affects males. They are not stimulated by the appearance of men, so they cannot fathom how men are affected.

Parents have a right to monitor the type of music being played in the home.

But the word is *monitor*. Accept as a fact that if you try to restrict a teen from listening to the music of his generation, he's going to break loose.

Parents have the right to set up rules regarding dating.

Parents should grant the privilege of dating only after they have examined such facts as age, dependability, willingness to accept responsibility, and mature behaviour.

During the early teen years it is better for teens not to pair off or date singly.

Teen dating

Families can provide opportunities for young people to establish healthy friendships without moving into single dating. Families can get together at one another's homes, plan trips, set out on picnics, go skating together, or foster any number of activities that allow young people to mix under controlled circumstances.

Dating and sexual behaviour

Parents unknowingly set up roadblocks of unacceptance so that teens find these two important areas the most difficult of all to discuss with their parents. Parents are well equipped with good intentions but faulty methods. By refusing to talk about the topic, they hope to discourage early dating.

Communicate.

Dating standards

Even during early teen years dating standards should be a frequent topic of family worship and discussion. Young people should feel free to make any statement and ask any question as shocking or adverse as they might be. The parent should avoid responding with lectures, put-downs, or any form of retribution.

Learning and growing conferences

Parents should organise learning and growing conferences for their teens. Perspectives may differ. Teens may overstate their views. Parents may overstate their objections. But lines of communication must be kept open.

A word for discouraged parents

Feelings of inadequacy are widespread among parents of teens. Tensions and disagreements may distress you. Remember: they *do* indicate that the channels of communication are open.

Firm, yet loving

Regardless of how difficult your teen may be, keep open the doors of acceptance, love and communication. Be firm, yet loving. Your teen may be hostile, bitter, rebellious, sullen, and unresponsive.

Remember: the more difficult the child, the more he needs your love and concern.

Never reject

A teen may reject every effort you put forth, but you must never reject him. You are the mature one; this difficult child is the immature one. Act in a firm but loving manner, no matter how traumatic the circumstances.

God cares

The Bible shows that God values persons in spite of their failures. Your worth and identity are not dependent upon what you have or have not accomplished as a parent. *Appreciate your own worth!*

Your child is a person of worth, even though he may have chosen different values from what you would have him choose.

Value

Parents must remember that
there is a person of worth
behind the most objectionable
behaviour. Behaviour is only a
symptom of a troubled teen
who is unable to cope with
the pressures of life.

God does not ignore our
behaviour, but he does not
reject us based on our behaviour.

Rest in the Lord

Psalm 37 may help a struggling parent survive. You will find great comfort during the trying periods of your children's adolescence if you can lean on a higher Power. But never forget that it isn't the number of prayers that makes the difference to a youth. Rather it is the difference that praying makes to our own attitudes which will speak to his heart.

God loves you and your teen with an everlasting love.